philanthropy's new passing gear:

Mission-Related Investing

A Policy and Implementation Guide for Foundation Trustees

Steven Godeke with Doug Bauer

© 2008, Rockefeller Philanthropy Advisors

table of contents

foreword

Without a doubt, the field of philanthropy is experiencing change — and in dramatic fashion. There are more donors, more resources, more ideas and more partners than even a decade ago. One of the most interesting dynamics is that the language and execution of philanthropy have embraced the principles and concepts of the private sector. The desire to generate positive impact has become paramount in the boardrooms of private foundations across the U.S. and around the world. The discipline of business thinking appears to enhance the effectiveness of non-governmental organizations and to achieve positive outcomes for communities and society at large.

Given this shift in thinking, it is not a surprise that we are seeing a growing interest among trustees and foundation leaders in mission-related investing (MRI). With over $600 billion in the endowments of U.S. private foundations, it is logical to consider how these funds can be put to use beyond generating income for grantmaking and begin to be a catalyst for social change via investments in market-driven entities.

As we talk with our peers and colleagues, we have seen the need for a practical publication that can inform decision-makers in philanthropy about how to move forward and implement an agenda for MRI in their institutions. With this guide, *Philanthropy's New Passing Gear: Mission-Related Investing,* plus other research that has been collected on MRI, there is now a strong body of work that can provide donors, trustees, staff of foundations, and the tax, legal and financial advisors that support them, with the data and advice they need to add this component to the mission and work of their foundations. At RPA, we truly see mission-related investing as a natural extension of thoughtful and effective philanthropy. We hope that you do too.

Kevin P.A. Broderick,
Chair, Board of Directors

Melissa A. Berman,
President and Chief Executive Officer

Rockefeller Philanthropy Advisors
February 2008

acknowledgements

The authors wish to thank everyone who helped us in putting this publication together. Over the course of 2007, the authors spoke with numerous colleagues about the guide and its contents. We are grateful for the formal and informal assistance we received along the way. But without a doubt, this guide would not have been possible without the outstanding advice and feedback of an advisory committee we convened to ensure that the guide was thoroughly vetted by a cross-section of legal, financial and grantmaking professionals.

We offer a special thanks to these individuals:
- Jed Emerson, Senior Fellow, Generation Foundation;
- John Goldstein, Managing Director, Imprint Capital Advisors;
- David Haas, Chair, The William Penn Foundation;
- Charly and Lisa Kleissner, Co-founders, The KL Felicitas Foundation;
- Robin Krause, Partner, Patterson Belknap Webb & Tyler LLP;
- Leslie Lowe, Chair, The Jessie Smith Noyes Foundation;
- Mary Jane McQuillen, Director, ClearBridge Advisors Legg Mason;
- Mary Jo Mullan, Vice President, The F.B. Heron Foundation;
- Karen Payne, President, Pacific Edge Investment Management;
- Ron Phillips, President & CEO, Coastal Enterprises Inc.;
- Raúl Pomares, Vice President, Guggenheim Partners;
- John Powers, Trustee, Educational Foundation of America;
- Luther Ragin, Jr., Vice President, The F.B. Heron Foundation;
- Stephen Toben, President, Flora Family Foundation; and
- John Townsend, Trustee, Altman Foundation.

Along with the advisory committee, we also received valuable input from our colleagues who helped us develop the case studies and provide comments. We wish to thank Paul Bradley, Julie Eades, Kate Guedj, Lisa Hagerman, Rosanne Haggerty, Tessa Hebb, Jason Malkin, Noni Ramos, Tom Reis, Michael Riley, Mary Anne Rodgers, Kate Starr, Rien van Gendt, Michael Weinstein, Karen Whalen, George Wilson, Jason Winship, and Richard Woo. Our thanks to these peers for their commitment to quality and clarity. It has helped our final product immensely.

The authors received strong editorial support from Chris Page, Lauren Russell Geskos, Karen Perry and Melinda Tuan of Rockefeller Philanthropy Advisors. The book was beautifully designed by Reid Smith of art270.

We would like to extend special thanks to William M. Dietel, Sharon King and Luther Ragin, Jr. of The F.B. Heron Foundation; Steve Toben of the Flora Family Foundation; and Alexandra Christy, Stuart Davidson and the trustees of the Woodcock Foundation. Without their enthusiasm and support, this publication would not have been possible. We are grateful for their commitment to mission-related investing and to broadly disseminating its potential to as wide an audience as possible.

Finally, please let us know what you think. Please send any comments or feedback to info@rockpa.org. We hope you find the guide useful and meaningful to the important work of creating, generating and sustaining positive social and environmental change in your community and around the world.

— Steven Godeke and Doug Bauer

introduction

Nineteen years ago the late Paul Ylvisaker wrote an essay entitled *Small Can Be Effective* that was published by the Council on Foundations. The monograph's target audience was the trustees and staff of foundations that did not have, at that time, the resources of a Rockefeller, MacArthur, Kellogg or Packard Foundation. The assets controlled by the intended audience were in the millions, not the billions.

Ylvisaker had been a philanthropic professional with both large and small foundations. He was a program executive at the Ford Foundation in the 1960s and for years he sat on the boards of family foundations in the U.S. and abroad. He also clearly understood the intersection between the nonprofit and public sectors for he had served in city and state government in Philadelphia and New Jersey.

In 1989, he was the Charles William Eliot Professor of Education (and former Dean) at the Graduate School of Education at Harvard and was a senior consultant at the Council on Foundations. While *Small Can Be Effective* was modest in scope (it still can be purchased from the Council for $5.00), the ideas Ylvisaker wrote about were big.

"Philanthropy took on the structured character and law of the corporate world and associated itself with the outlook and professionalism of organized science," wrote Ylvisaker. "It dedicated itself to finding systemic solutions to underlying causes of poverty and other social ills, and over time, has become a recognized social process — in effect, a set of private legislatures defining public problems, setting goals and priorities, and allocating resources toward the general good. Foundations have, in effect, been given a 'hunting license' as private organizations to participate in what has conventionally been thought of as exclusively a public/governmental domain." Ylvisaker goes on in the essay to cite 20 ways small foundations can be effective beyond the grants that they give to worthy nonprofits. Three of the ways were "Lending," "Insuring," and "Investing." As was typical of Ylvisaker, he was ahead of his time.

Another phrase that Ylvisaker used was that philanthropy was "society's passing gear," by which he meant philanthropic resources should be used to fund and accelerate new ideas, new methods, and new programs that can change the way we as a society serve and help others.

That was 1989. This is 2008. What has changed? Not much and, indeed, quite a lot.

Many of the problems that troubled us then in the U.S. still trouble us now. To mention just a few:
• Poor public education in U.S. urban communities;
• Inadequate delivery of proper healthcare;
• Shortsighted development patterns which generate sprawl and pollution; and
• A lack of serious investment in poor neighborhoods and communities in urban and rural settings.

In the developing world, the list of problems is long and sad:
• Tens of millions impacted by HIV/AIDS;
• Billions with little or no access to clean water;
• Almost ten million children dying annually of diseases that are preventable with current vaccines or drug therapies;
• Environmental degradation on a massive scale through climate change and loss of biodiversity; and
• Billions of people still living on less than $2 a day.

What has changed a lot is the context in which U.S. philanthropy operates. Since 1989, we have seen a dramatic growth in philanthropy from 25,000 private foundations to over 72,000 foundations today with assets of $600 billion. That kind of money generates some $30 billion in grants each year, according to the 2006 figures from *Giving USA*. There has also been an explosion of philanthropy in Europe and Asia.

We have also seen significant growth in the number of nonprofits. There are 1.5 million nonprofits in the U.S. working on a myriad of issues and causes. Despite this increase, determining how to solve problems, drive change or discover answers through these nonprofits is more complicated than ever.

Against this backdrop, philanthropists are acknowledging that they can no longer rely on the model of investigating a problem, funding a solution, and then turning the solution over to the public sector for scale and true societal impact. Public resources are limited and will probably become even more so as demographics, politics and increased pressure on our planet's limited resources influence what governments here or abroad can or cannot fund or support or sustain.

We have also realized that market-based solutions are sometimes better than government solutions. This has, indeed, happened both in the U.S. and Europe as well as in the developing world.

While the work of private foundations draws more scrutiny from the media, legislators and regulators, the work has become harder and more fluid. The old models may still work, but will they make a difference? How can private foundations of all sizes be more nimble in their work and demonstrate real results in the issues or communities they care about?

Some private foundation trustees, grantmaking professionals, investment managers and advisors, tax-exempt lawyers and others are advocating for the field of organized philanthropy to change and incorporate new ways of thinking and operating. They advocate for transformation because they believe that philanthropy needs to do a better job of generating positive social change. They advocate because they believe traditional grantmaking by itself is no longer enough. It is not enough because of the limitations of the traditional charity model. The answer to every problem is not a grant. If the foundation community desires greater impact — and more entrepreneurial approaches to problem solving or generating social capital — then it is time to consider additional approaches.

One of the most exciting of these new approaches is mission-related investing or MRI. Mission-related investing, broadly defined, encompasses any investment activity which seeks to generate a positive social or environmental impact in addition to providing a financial return.

Why Mission-Related Investing? Why Now?

In January of last year, *The Los Angeles Times* published a series of articles focusing on the Bill and Melinda Gates Foundation and what the newspaper perceived as the disconnect between the philanthropic mission of the foundation and its investment policies. But how does a foundation create consistency — or synergy or alignment — between its program and investment activities?

In parallel, another force was gathering steam. After many years of thinking, researching, testing and investing, the idea of mission-related investing was emerging. It was put plain in a 2005 report by one of the pioneers in MRI, Luther Ragin, Jr., Vice President of The F.B. Heron Foundation. He described how Heron's board of directors embraced mission-related investment by simply asking: "Should a private foundation be more than a private investment company that uses some of its excess cash flow for charitable purposes?" The answer to that concise but provocative question should be "yes," but how to answer the questions that follow is not easy and moving to implementation is complicated. It is complicated because across the landscape of the some 72,000 private foundations there is not an accepted standard operating model. Most foundations in the U.S. are family governed and managed. Less than 5,000 foundations have professional staff. Within the large, well-known private foundations with staffs, a wide gulf exists between program and investment staff.

In the boardroom, private foundation trustees struggle with a need to achieve an ongoing annual return on investment of 9% to maintain and grow the private foundation and its corpus. For those foundations seeking to sustain their assets in perpetuity, the math is straightforward: 5% for grants and qualifying administrative expenses; 1% for investment fees; and 3% to stay ahead of inflation. To achieve such a return in good years and bad is not easy. The perception of diverting attention or energy from an investment discipline that achieves such returns is difficult to do — especially when wise and well-paid investment managers and consultants strongly discourage it.

And yet, some trustees are intellectually and emotionally attracted to the idea of how market-based solutions could be a way to tackle program challenges. They would like to know how their foundations can support (and even prosper from) the creativity of entrepreneurs building triple bottom line firms which benefit investors, society and the environment and how nonprofit organizations with more diverse capital structures may be supported in achieving greater scale in their work. They see how these approaches can be an extension of the foundation's mission and program, rather than a substitute for them.

The worry is, however, whether the clarion call is coming from a siren. It is not. The push-pull that trustees struggle with regarding mission-related investing is one that is informed by values. And values drive most, if not all, philanthropic decisions. But how can values inform the financial or investment decisions of a private foundation?

"There is an idea that values are divided between the financial and the societal, but this is a fundamentally wrong way to view how we create value," writes Jed Emerson, Senior Fellow at the Generation Foundation and a long-time proponent of MRI. "Value is whole. The world is not divided into corporate bad guys and social heroes."

We would argue that values should inform investment decisions. Mission-related investing is an extension of how donors and their foundations can do thoughtful and effective philanthropy, but how to execute such a strategy is daunting — even for the most sophisticated organizations. A roadmap is needed to help translate these concepts, ideas and philosophy into policies and practices that will create an MRI strategy and program at your foundation.

From Idea to Execution

While a large body of work has evolved around concepts such as program-related investments, proxy voting and shareholder resolutions, socially responsible investing, double/triple bottom line investing, and blended value investing, few resources exist for private foundation trustees and staff who commit to adopt an MRI program and integrate it with the existing policies, processes and workflows of their organizations.

There is also little sharing of the structures or risk allocation tools used in MRI transactions. Investors and social entrepreneurs face ongoing legal, tax and organizational hurdles. Expertise remains largely sector and program specific. For example, community development investors remain unfamiliar with structures used by environmental investors and vice versa. Best practices are changing rapidly with the proliferation of investment options and strategies.

The goal of this guide is to provide foundation trustees and, where or when appropriate, staff with a process to create both an overall policy for MRI as well as specific paths for implementation. Our mission-related investing roadmap outlines how to:

- Ground a strategy within the values and mission of your foundation;
- Understand the various catalysts for MRI within a foundation;
- Structure a policy discussion in the boardroom;
- Integrate MRI into existing program and investment processes;
- Link your investment asset allocation with your program goals;

- Determine the appropriate MRI investment tools and strategies for the foundation;
- Select appropriate financial, program and investment consultants;
- Organize the board, and staff and investment consultants to find, evaluate, approve and execute MRI investment vehicles;
- Monitor investment performance of an MRI portfolio; and ultimately
- Integrate social returns into the ongoing investment and program decisions of the foundation.

We have also included 12 case studies which reflect the diversity of experiences of foundations active in MRI. The core audience of this guide is donors, foundation trustees and executive and program staff — those who have the authority to establish strategies and policies and implement new ideas. At the same time, we recognize that institutional investors, wealthy individuals and families, tax/financial/legal advisors, as well as the trustees and staff of higher education and nonprofit hospital endowments will be interested in the guide. We invite and welcome their interest in mission-related investing.

Mission-related investing is an idea and a force whose time has come in the field of philanthropy. It is an idea with historical roots. Here is just one example: In 1918, the Carnegie Foundation for the Advancement of Teaching realized that professors were retiring with little to no savings after lifetimes devoted to educating others. With a $1 million gift from the Carnegie Corporation of New York, a life insurance company was incorporated and dedicated to providing life insurance and pensions for college and university employees. That organization is known today as TIAA-CREF — one of the world's largest retirement systems investing over $400 billion on behalf of over 3.2 million participants.

As we move further into the 21st century, private foundations must unleash more of their resources, not fewer, to achieve positive impacts that change communities and societies. To do that, means thinking beyond the five percent payout and considering all alternatives. Mission-related investing is an idea that adds value by creating value for all parties involved: communities, society, the marketplace and the foundation.

The only way to begin is to consider the possibilities and to act.

Chapter 1:

Setting the Ground Rules

Why, What and How: First Come Values and Mission

Any conversation about mission-related investing at your foundation should be firmly grounded in the core values and mission of your institution. By clearly articulating your values and mission, your organization's first steps in how to use mission-related investing will become clearer. Your values and mission can be explicit or implicit. Many organizations have formally established and articulated values and missions while some foundations have begun a set of philanthropic activities without formally developing explicit values and mission statements. Regardless of where your organization is within this process, it will be useful to consider the following questions as a way to anchor your thoughts and make certain assumptions more explicit:

Values and Motivation: Why are you interested in philanthropy and community involvement? Traditions, mentors, personal interests and experiences, faith and spirituality, social change and volunteering, business skills and experience.

Many donors name fairness, compassion and justice as their primary motivations. Within large institutional philanthropies and multi-generational family foundations, the board and staff may look to the founder's values when seeking to find or define appropriate program interests.

Mission and Objectives: What are you trying to accomplish?
Make a difference, give back, leave a legacy, create a vehicle for working with your family, express your values and explore your interests, use your talents and skills for a different purpose, support the people and institutions which have been important to you.

Operational Goals: How would you like to be involved in and manage your philanthropy? Hands-on management, formal or informal management structures, planning or spontaneity, consensus or donor-driven decision-making, perpetuity or limited period for foundation, collaborative or independent, seek out grantees or respond to proposals.

Tactics: What is your giving style and/or discipline, and what are your giving interests? Issues or institutions, special projects or operating costs, more or less risk, immediate crisis or root causes, leveraging other funders or going alone, ongoing support or financial self-sufficiency?[1]

The goal of this guide is to help you determine how mission-related investment can fit into your organization's values and mission — and help leverage greater value for you regardless of your specific area of interest.

Values and Mission Statements

Building on the values of your organization, this questioning process can lead to the creation of formal values and mission statements. Considering values and mission is a useful first step in an ongoing cycle of engagement and education. This cycle continues with the selection of your method of giving and investing, and the establishment of appropriate philanthropic and investment entities. Once you begin implementing and executing your strategies, you can then evaluate your results and refine your strategies in an ongoing cycle.

A Philanthropic Cycle of Engagement and Education

Source: Rockefeller Philanthropy Advisors

Values, Mission and Investment: The Russell Family Foundation (TRFF)

The Russell Family Foundation was endowed by Jane and George Russell in 2000 upon the sale of their pioneering pension fund consulting business, the Frank Russell Company. TRFF currently has assets of approximately $150 million. The foundation's core values are integrity, mutual trust, constructive communications, life-long learning, and courage. The Russell Family Foundation's mission is to contribute to innovative community impact, build quality relationships with partners, and to maintain an outstanding work culture. In 2006, TRFF awarded grants totaling $13.5 million in three funding programs focused:

• Locally in Pierce County, Washington, on grassroots leadership development;

• Regionally in Western Washington on environmental sustainability; and

• Globally on peace and security.

As an entrepreneurial organization with its roots in financial services, TRFF chose to focus on the process and analytics of integrating mission-related investment into its overall strategy and operations. "We understood that we would not have the most assets, but we could seek to lead by following a rigorous process and sharing this with other foundations," said Richard Woo, TRFF CEO. This approach also addressed the philosophical diversity among the family and non-family board members regarding mission-related investing.

In 2004, TRFF began a $1 million pilot program funded from its endowment for MRI opportunities and allocated the necessary staff and board time to explore MRI policies. This initial pilot resulted in the following investment activities:

• An investment in the Vanguard Calvert Social Index Fund (a screened public equity mutual fund);

- The purchase of a certificate of deposit with Shorebank Pacific in Ilwaco, Washington, a community bank which lends to environmentally sustainable businesses — Shorebank Pacific was also a grantee of TRFF;
- TRFF signing the Carbon Disclosure Project, which is an institutional investor initiative calling on the world's largest corporations to disclose their carbon emissions and their strategies to manage climate change risk;[2] and
- The adoption of an investment policy statement incorporating mission-related investments.[3]

In 2005, the mission-related investment program was expanded to $7 million and has since made additional investments in screened funds and created an allocation for clean tech venture capital. TRFF is now monitoring the votes of its shareholder proxies through Institutional Shareholder Services (ISS) and is directly exercising its proxy votes on specific companies in its portfolio. For example, TRFF supported a 2006 shareholder resolution for sustainability reporting at Wal-Mart. TRFF's board assesses the impact of particular proxy votes in the same way they would evaluate the potential impact of a grant. TRFF has also completed two program-related investments (PRIs): a loan to Enterprise Community Partners, Inc. for green affordable housing around Puget Sound and a loan to the Interra Project for sustainable economics.

After three years, TRFF is sharing its experience with other funders which may be philosophically committed to mission-related investing but are not yet clear on the how-to. The foundation has seen great value in integrating its program and investing goals. "MRI is becoming a two-way street where we are beginning to apply more social and philosophical due diligence to our investing and more financial rigor to our grantmaking," said Richard Woo.

From Defining Values to Creating Value: Philanthropic Strategy & Tactics

Through their role as the institutional bedrock of the civic sector, U.S. foundations have had an extraordinarily positive impact. As Joel Fleishman states in his book, *The Foundation: A Great American Secret,*[4] "the American civic sector, of which our many foundations are an integral part, is a wonder of the world and an unprecedented social phenomenon." From their privileged perch, foundations should be the driving force of "greater good" with regard to charitable giving and social entrepreneurship. Foundations can operate free from the political pressure of the public sector and the short time horizons facing corporations. Michael Porter and Mark Kramer[5] have framed value creation by foundations in the following way:

> *"Foundations are in the business of contributing to society by using scarce philanthropic resources to their maximum potential. A foundation creates value when it achieves an equivalent social benefit with fewer dollars or creates greater social benefit for comparable cost. A foundation's strategy depends upon the selection of a unique position; therefore, the starting point for a foundation's strategy is to limit the number of social challenges which it will address."*

Foundations typically work through others by providing grants and create additional value when their activities generate social benefits beyond the value of their grants. A foundation can accomplish this in four ways:

• Selecting the best grantees, and measuring the foundation's own performance to improve future selections;

- Signaling to other funders through education and matching grants;
- Improving the performance of grant recipients by moving from passive capital provider to fully engaged partner; and
- Advancing the state of knowledge and practice.

The core question becomes: "How can your foundation create the greatest value, given everything you know about your foundation's culture, passions, expertise, and resources, about what other funders have done or are doing, and about the problems you wish to address?"

Constructing a Philanthropic Infrastructure

Building on the values, mission and strategy of your philanthropy, you can select from a wide range of legal and financial entities to realize your goals. In addition to using traditional philanthropic structures such as private foundations, donor-advised funds and charitable remainder trusts, donors are utilizing legal entities such as family limited partnerships and limited liability corporations to make their mission-related investments. Establishing a structure which does not impede your grantmaking and investment activities is essential and should consider the fact that your goals may change over time. Prior to establishing these legal entities, considering the following questions is important:

- Have you provided clear guidance to legal and financial advisors about what you envision?
- Have you defined a mission that is broad enough so that it will endure as long as there is money to fund it?

- Have you structured your philanthropy in a way that best achieves your tax and other financial objectives?
- Do you understand the "ground rules" well enough to know that you can be comfortable operating within them?
- Have you created a system of checks and balances to ensure that the foundation fulfills its charitable mission and remains in compliance with applicable laws?[6]

   The decision to fund your philanthropy through an outright gift, the establishment of a charitable trust, or by using private assets to make direct mission-related investments will depend on timing, financial, and personal considerations. The choice of a particular philanthropic legal vehicle (e.g. a private foundation, donor-advised fund, supporting organization, or

A Framework for Philanthropy and Mission-Related Investing

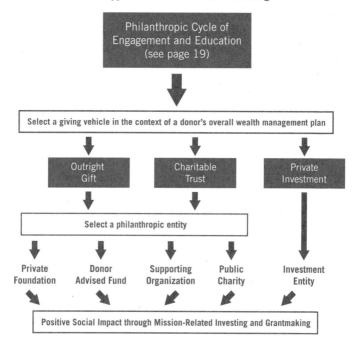

Source: Rockefeller Philanthropy Advisors

Chapter 1: Setting the Ground Rules

public charity) should consider your desire to maintain control of the assets, the type of assets you will be contributing, and the discretion you want to maintain over your grantmaking and investments.

Caveat: Sound Program & Investment Practices as Prerequisite

Organizations with good governance practices and strong agreement among the board and staff on program and investment strategies are the best candidates for mission-related investing. Mission-related investing is no substitute for clearly articulated investment and program policies. In fact, MRI will add new dimensions to the investment and program challenges you already face. A mission-related investing strategy should be incorporated within your overall asset allocation and reflect the diversification and correlation assumptions of that allocation. As John Powers of The Educational Foundation of America (www.efaw.org) stated, "the impact of our overall portfolio asset allocation has dwarfed the effects of our mission-related investing on the performance of our portfolio."

---

1 *Adapted from Esposito, Virginia M. Editor et al,* Splendid Legacy, The Guide to Creating Your Family Foundation, *National Center for Family Philanthropy, 2002.*

2 *See www.cdproject.net for more information about the Carbon Disclosure Project.*

3 *See Appendix 1, for the MRI Investment Policy of the Jessie Smith Noyes Foundation which served as the basis for TRFF's investment policy.*

4 *Fleishman, Joel L.,* The Foundation: A Great American Secret: How Private Wealth is Changing the World, *PublicAffairs, 2007.*

5 *Porter, Michael E. and Mark R. Kramer, "Philanthropy's New Agenda: Creating Value,"* Harvard Business Review, *November–December 1999, pp. 121-130.*

6 *Adapted from Sare, John, "Facing Important Legal Issues," in Esposito et al,* Splendid Legacy, The Guide to Creating Your Family Foundation, *National Center for Family Philanthropy, 2002.*

Chapter 2:

Deciding to Act: Triggers for Change

Like any significant organizational change, considering and/or introducing mission-related investing can have a broad range of causes. While individual reasons and triggers will vary among foundations, they generally fall into the following categories:

Ethical Imperative

Many organizations begin mission-related investing based on the strict ethical values of the organization — without the assumption that MRI will necessarily lead to financial returns or organizational effectiveness. This ethical imperative may arise from awareness that there is an underlying inconsistency between the grantmaking and investment activities of the foundation. For example, a foundation finds it is providing grant support to community activists while at the same time investing in corporations which the activists are targeting for reform. This inconsistency may be brought into focus by trustees, staff, grantees or outside attention. While contemporary examples abound, foundations and endowments grappling with how to connect their philanthropy and their investments is not a new phenomenon. For example, Trinity Church on Wall Street was exposed in the press as the owner of some of New York City's worst slums on the Lower East Side — in 1908. By 1910, Trinity succumbed to outside pressure and changed its real estate investment policy.[7]

Value Creation and Efficient Resource Management

As foundations seek to maximize their positive social impact, many have become aware of the limits of the traditional "two-pocket philanthropy" model in which an organization's financial resources are managed in isolation from its grantmaking activities. A desire to find ways to harness all of a foundation's assets which are not distributed in grants has created the impetus for many institutions to explore mission-related investing as a means to increase their organizational effectiveness. Foundation trustees may have a sense that greater impact could be accomplished through additional uses of the foundation's assets. In other words, grants are not the only tool available to a foundation, and in certain circumstances, mission-related investing may be an effective complement, or simply a more effective way to achieve the desired outcome. Indeed, this can move foundations beyond the old adage of "If you only have a hammer, every problem looks like a nail."

Relationship Building

As a foundation seeks new ways to deepen its connections to individual grantees, investees and the communities in which it operates, mission-related investing can be a highly effective channel to build these relationships. For example, program-related investments such as low-interest loans can dramatically increase the capital available to high-performance nonprofits. Community foundations in particular can demonstrate their commitment and expertise to their communities by providing donors, institutional investors and individuals with MRI opportunities such as local or regional loan funds which national donor-advised funds do not offer.

Reflection of Who We Are

Many donors see a direct link between their own history and identity and their philanthropic activities. If a donor has created wealth through entrepreneurial activities, she or he may be attracted to mission-related investing as a philanthropic model which reflects her or his previous experience in the private sector. Concepts such as financial self-sufficiency and accountability resonate with these donors. For example, Pierre Omidyar, who created eBay with the goal of empowering small buyers and sellers, has structured his philanthropy to break down the boundaries between the nonprofit and business worlds. Within family foundations, inter-generational discussions may trigger a reassessment of the foundation's objectives. The next generation may seek to expand the philanthropic toolkit to include mission-related investing, but needs to place MRI in a context which is understandable to the current generation. As one family member stated, "my father — who is a businessman — opposed any kind of mission-related investing until we presented a microfinance investment as an entrepreneurial opportunity to alleviate poverty — which had been the primary focus of our grantmaking to that point."

Investment Attractiveness

Some institutions may see MRI as a way to identify and mitigate the long-term risks of major societal issues such as human rights, climate change and environmental degradation. In addition to managing these risks, MRI can also generate profitable opportunities, e.g., solar power and clean technology investments and strong corporate governance, which can lead to higher investment performance for their organizations.

Breaking Boundaries:
The Omidyar Network

Pierre Omidyar, the founder of eBay, began his philanthropy through his private foundation and supported several entrepreneurial nonprofits. However, in 2004, he dissolved his for-profit private investment office, and combined it with his foundation. This new entity, Omidyar Network (www.omidyar.net), can fund from three sources: a for-profit entity for investments, another for-profit entity for overhead, and a 501(c)(3) non-profit entity for traditional foundation activities. The goal of the network is to align strategic philanthropy, socially responsible investing and sustainable business. Omidyar had found for-profits that advanced social goals like nonprofits, and nonprofits that earned money like for-profits, and he wanted to create a model which would allow him to effectively support these hybrid organizations.

After meeting Muhammad Yunus, the Nobel Prize-winning founder of the Grameen Bank, Omidyar became convinced that microfinance was such a business model. The Omidyar Network's major focus now is to commercialize microfinance and to have for-profit capital be a tool for good.[8]

Tactical Opportunities

Many foundations have taken the philosophical steps to consider mission-related investment, but only take action when a concrete opportunity appears on the horizon. A worthwhile investment opportunity may come up, and your foundation would like to participate. A strategic planning process has surfaced the idea of expanding your philanthropic toolkit, and the board is now prepared to act.

All of these mission-related investing catalysts have the common thread of strong internal champions who move the idea forward. Board-level champions with the ability to convince other board members and staff (if you have them) to begin to integrate the foundation's investment and program activities appear to be the most effective means of placing MRI on the board's agenda.

Threshold Issue: Fiduciary Duty

Once MRI is raised as a serious option, trustees may turn their attention to the fiduciary and tax implications. A growing body of literature is addressing these issues.[9] Simply stated, the trustees of a foundation have a fiduciary relationship to the organization and thus owe fundamental duties of care, loyalty, and good faith to the corporation. The duty of care requires that a trustee carry out his or her responsibilities with the level of care that a prudent person would use in similar circumstances. The duty of loyalty requires that trustees put the interests of the corporation first and protect the best interests of the corporation, including the duty to act only in good faith and in the best interests of the corporation. A third duty is the duty of obedience which requires that trustees remain true to the purposes and legal structure of the organization.

When considering mission-related investing, the trustees' decisions must be made subject to these duties. In addition, foundation trustees must take into account the particular tax rules that govern MRI activities, specifically the "jeopardy investment rules" which provide that a foundation may only invest in a manner that does not imperil its ability to carry on its exempt purposes. The relevant standard is that foundation managers must take care to provide for the long and short term financial needs of the foundation. In doing so, the trustees are permitted to use a portfolio wide analysis.

Traditionally, when overseeing the investment activities, foundation trustees have seen their duty as being to maximize the risk-adjusted return of the foundation's diversified portfolio. Any deviation from this approach could create concerns as to how prudently the trustee was acting to protect the foundation's interests. This standard has evolved over time to incorporate new investment options such as private equity and hedge funds which were considered too risky a few years ago. The fiduciary standards applied by a foundation trustee are also somewhat different than those applied to other types of endowments and pension funds where there are third party interests and other interests at play. Foundation trustees have more discretion to incorporate non-financial considerations such as a donor's wishes or the charitable purposes of the foundation.

In thinking about MRIs, trustees may be considering "program-related investments" (PRIs) among the options. PRIs are defined by the tax code as an exception to the jeopardy investment rules described above. Investments that qualify as program-related investments are considered to be charitable expenditures, the same as a grant. PRIs and other types of MRI activities do not necessarily create any fiduciary issues in terms of prudent management of the assets, so long as the trustees' decisions satisfy their basic fiduciary responsibilities to the foundation in the overall management of the assets.

PRIs must satisfy specific criteria because of their special treatment by the foundation as grants which count toward the foundation's annual payout obligation. They must satisfy three criteria: (i) the investment's primary purpose must be to advance the foundation's charitable objectives; (ii) neither the production of income nor the appreciation of property can be a significant purpose; and (iii) the funds cannot be used directly or indirectly for lobbying or political purposes. Many foundations have equated mission-related investing with program-related investing while others distinguish between below-market PRIs and market-rate MRIs.

For mission-related investments which are not PRIs, trustees need to be able to answer the following questions:
• How can I consider the social and environmental consequences of an investment in addition to its risk-adjusted financial return when evaluating investment opportunities?
• How do these investments fit within the foundation's overall asset allocation?

Although you should consult your legal advisors to get comfortable with your organization's specific consideration of fiduciary duty and mission-related investment, there are foundations that have successfully addressed these issues and are building mission-related portfolios without violating their fiduciary obligations.

Beyond the Single Champion: Policy Discussion in the Boardroom

An individual advocate in an organization, no matter how well-placed, can not implement a mission-related investing strategy without broad board support. Board education is critical at this point, and outside experts can play a central role in providing the requisite knowledge. Many organizations let the idea percolate over three or four board meetings to surface questions and concerns. Surveying the landscape and talking to a range of other foundations, investors, existing grantees, and tax, legal, and investment advisors with relevant knowledge and expertise can provide new insights and highlight possible pitfalls.

It is critical that the champion does the necessary homework and works with board members to explain and demystify MRI. Trustees may be empowered by meeting with their peers on other foundation boards or representatives from other institutional investors such as public sector pension funds, insurance companies or banks. Such exchanges may also lead to collaborations with these organizations on future MRI transactions.

Once your board decides to proceed with mission-related investing, possible levels of engagement include:
• Providing a clear mandate to implement a broad MRI strategy;
• Working with existing grantees to determine how PRIs could assist them in meeting their mission goals;
• Establishing teams with staff and/or external experts to implement the strategy and develop the appropriate policies and procedures;

MassPRIM: Economically Targeted Investment at Public Pension Funds

Public and private pension funds, along with insurance companies and other institutional investors, are increasingly seeking to attract capital to underserved urban markets and build assets in low-income communities. Known as Economically Targeted Investment (ETI), these programs target market-rate returns against established benchmarks in addition to generating social benefits. The targeted investments of the pension funds, which have been established under intense public scrutiny, can serve as interesting comparables for foundations.

Since the early 1980s, Massachusetts has had a history of ETI programs based on the state pension fund's (MassPRIM) legislative mandate to invest in the Commonwealth whenever possible while still fulfilling its fiduciary duty.[10] In 2003, the Massachusetts state treasurer developed a formal ETI policy approved by the nine-member board that contains several best practice lessons of particular relevance for not only public pension funds but other institutional investors such as foundation boards pursuing market-rate mission related investment opportunities:

- In the case of MassPRIM, a board-level champion (the state treasurer) engaged objective outside experts to review ETIs and develop an ETI policy with a set of five investment selection criteria.
- The investment criteria were substantial, direct, and intended to first achieve market rates of return and secondly measurable benefits to the Massachusetts economy; in addition to targeting capital gaps such as in urban areas.
- After the policy was approved, the board champion followed up with staff to ensure that the policy was put into effect.

- An ETI request for proposal distributed in the marketplace made the bidding process transparent and deflected political interference.
- MassPRIM's ETIs are approved through an investment selection process that incorporates a rigorous investment philosophy. The ETI program fits into the pre-existing asset classes of fixed income, real estate, and alternatives; and tracks the corresponding benchmarks.
- ETI managers report on the financial returns and the collateral social benefits of these investments through an ETI Quarterly Report.

- Proceeding with a specific engagement activity such as voting proxies or screening the endowment's portfolio;
- Entering the market opportunistically through individual transactions; and
- Carving out a portion of the program budget or endowment to be used to make mission-related investments.

Incremental approaches, such as carving out a dedicated amount from the endowment or using program funds to experiment in mission-related investing, may be viewed by your board as lower risk and more prudent. In fact, more comprehensive strategies may accelerate the introduction of mission-related investing throughout the organization. Many foundations start with a set amount or percentage of their assets for mission-related investing, while others may just react to opportunities. Some foundations have decided to first develop an overall asset allocation and then to seek mission-related investments across those asset classes rather than to view mission-related investing as a separate asset class.

The long-term goal is to have MRI encompass all of a foundation's assets and to maximize the use of this highly effective complement to grantmaking. The path to that long-term goal is as varied as the foundations themselves. The point is to begin and pick a path and speed that is most appropriate for your foundation.

Implementation & the Investment Committee

Foundation boards typically delegate financial oversight duties to an investment committee, which works with the internal investment staff and external investment advisors. While the investment committee members should have a broad knowledge of investment, they should also understand the program goals of the foundation. In some organizations, the investment committee may operate separately from the "program-driven" board — a structure which supports the assumption that effective money management enables grantmaking but should be kept in isolation from it. Mission-related investment strategies require tighter coordination of the program and investment activities of the board.

Communications and Culture

The board is the most powerful voice in the organization and will need to be directly engaged in the introduction of an MRI strategy to the staff. Organizations are typically quite sensitive to board mandates; therefore, how the board communicates this new strategy will be critical to its success or failure. The communications goal will be for the organization to think of MRI as an integral tool for its work in achieving positive results — not an isolated add-on function. Mission-related investment will elicit questions, and the board and staff should be able to speak about the new strategy to internal audiences as well as outside investment consultants and managers and your grantees. You should also acknowledge that introducing MRI will bring cultural and organizational change to your foundation. You will need to anticipate a reluctance, and even resistance from staff and advisors who may feel threatened by these changes. Mission-related investing should redefine everyone's job, and may not play to the staff's traditional strengths and training. The goal is to build awareness of the linkages between investment and program and the necessity for a coordinated approach.

Building the MRI Team: Who Comes to the First Meeting?

Active participation by both program and investment staff as well as strong board support will be essential to your success. Tactics vary widely among foundations and range from establishing a free-standing, dedicated mission-related investment team to completely integrating program and investment staff. The bridging skills needed to combine keen financial analysis with program objectives appear to be scarce in most foundations. Many foundations bring all mission-related investment decisions to the investment committee as a means to highlight the importance of bridging mission and investment and strengthening internal relationships.

A central challenge is how to build out the needed skills, while acknowledging that mission-related investing is just one part of the responsibilities of both program and investment staff. Some organizations have internal experts who work with program staff to identify transactions and lead the transaction through closing. This may be a dedicated mission-related investment staff person or legal counsel with experience in documenting and closing transactions. One foundation president, who was launching a mission-related investing strategy, recruited his CFO to lead the effort, thereby making him an advocate rather than a potential hindrance. Family-led and/or smaller and newer foundations may be more nimble with mission-related investing, simply because they do not have large, independent program and investment teams with long histories of working in isolation from each other. Over time, you may find that the qualifications which you seek in hiring staff will change significantly. A key element will be to build mutual trust and respect between these two worlds.

W.K. Kellogg Foundation's Mission-Driven Investments: Experiment at Scale

The W.K. Kellogg Foundation has recently announced plans to invest $100 million of its $9 billion endowment in "mission-driven investments" in the U.S. and Africa. $25 million has been allocated to further social and economic transformation in rural southern Africa. In the U.S., Kellogg expects to concentrate its $75 million investment on vulnerable children through investments in education and small- and medium-enterprise development.

While the Kellogg Foundation has made great strides funding and supporting programs to achieve its mission and goals, its board and staff knew they could not always help their partners realize scale and sustainability solely through grantmaking dollars. Both board and staff felt they needed investment tools in addition to grants to support at least some of their partner organizations' work. For some time there had been internal discussions about how to better leverage Kellogg's endowment for greater mission impact. The president and CEO, Sterling Speirn, and the board decided in early 2007 to take action.

The actual decision to approve a pilot mission-driven investing program was made very quickly. Just days after broaching the idea with the board in a conversation in January of 2007, a team was formed to do an intensive scan of the mission-related investment field. The team crossed boundaries within the foundation. It included both investment and program staff. Together, the team scanned who was doing double-bottom line investing (earning income on investments that also help achieve mission goals), and what they were learning. It looked at whether or not the foundation would find enough products and players across the asset classes to make such investment feasible. What the team found was both positive and confirming. The literature, which featured the results of others working in the field, showed that it was possible to recycle capital and preserve the endowment while driving greater mission impact.

continued

W.K. Kellogg Foundation's Mission-Driven Investments: Experiment at Scale *continued*

Sufficient deal opportunities existed in a range of asset classes, everything from bank deposits to equity funds, so any investment potentially could yield both sufficient earnings and learning for the foundation.

Some three months later, the results of the scan were shared with the board. Enthusiastic about the findings, the board agreed to allocate $100 million dollars for the experiment. Upon doing so, it asked the team to continue its work. Specifically, its members sought more detail on how the plan would be implemented, including governance, management, and monitoring.

By May, the team presented an implementation plan. The plan identified an investment focus for both the United States and southern Africa, as well as corresponding criteria. Careful to focus the pilot in the early stages of its development, the plan also recommended a simple governing structure that would ensure that due diligence was applied to all deals, while at the same time enabling the team to be responsive to emerging opportunities.

From the beginning, it was decided that the project would have a three-tiered structure consisting of: (i) the Board Finance Committee charged with governance and oversight, (ii) an Investment Committee with internal and external members responsible for strategy and deal decision making, and (iii) a Portfolio Management Team responsible for deal execution and portfolio management.

The foundation wanted to be able to rapidly prototype, test and adjust its strategy based upon real-time findings. The goal was to avoid "over thinking" the process.

In terms of action goals, the foundation decided that it wanted to meet a mix of below-market and market-rate benchmarks by asset class while achieving social impact. It also said it wanted a realistic plan for evaluating the pilot's performance. The foundation's staff is currently working on formulating metrics to determine whether or not the program successfully meets both its financial and social goals.

By early 2008, the foundation hopes to open the deal flow. Overall, its leadership is optimistic about the future of mission-driven investing at the Kellogg Foundation. As one staff member said, "Few ideas have resonated more completely or more quickly than helping to closely connect investments to our mission. We have the potential to add a significant new tool to our social change toolbox."

Toward that end, the Kellogg Foundation will be posting the details of its mission-driven investing plans, including deal criteria, on its website (www.wkkf.org).

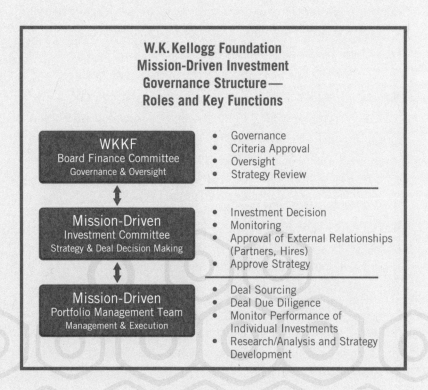

**W.K. Kellogg Foundation
Mission-Driven Investment
Governance Structure —
Roles and Key Functions**

WKKF
Board Finance Committee
Governance & Oversight

- Governance
- Criteria Approval
- Oversight
- Strategy Review

Mission-Driven
Investment Committee
Strategy & Deal Decision Making

- Investment Decision
- Monitoring
- Approval of External Relationships (Partners, Hires)
- Approve Strategy

Mission-Driven
Portfolio Management Team
Management & Execution

- Deal Sourcing
- Deal Due Diligence
- Monitor Performance of Individual Investments
- Research/Analysis and Strategy Development

Where Are the Right Advisors and Staff?

You may face the dilemma of wanting to implement an MRI strategy, and yet, not be able to find the appropriate expertise to lead you through the process of developing an investment policy statement which reflects your values. Your investment committee and internal investment staff have the challenge of managing relationships with an array of consultants, fund managers, investment portfolio managers and custodians — each with a potential interest in retaining the status quo. Board members may have professional and personal relationships at stake with these managers as well. A fully integrated MRI strategy will require your organization to unbundle the layers between the board and your institution's financial assets.

Traditional investment consultants may be aware of socially-screened funds, but may not have the appropriate skills to assess the broader universe of mission-related opportunities. However, some established pension and endowment investment consultants are now following their clients into the field of mission-related investing. Recent entrants have launched dedicated research units focusing primarily on sustainable investing and the implications of issues such as climate change on the investment performance. Building the right team of foundation staff, existing investment managers and MRI investment consultants is critical to your success.

It is challenging to find MRI investment consultants with the necessary skills to advise foundations on the financial and social dimensions of investments and assist in origination, structuring, and portfolio management. Most MRI consultants are specialized in particular asset classes or approaches such as screening or environmental investments. This can preclude them from providing neutral advice. Many foundation boards and investment committees find that developing a request for proposal (RFP) for a mission-related investment consultant is a good first step. By presenting your MRI strategy as a clear client mandate to outside investment consultants and managers, your organization will be better able to find the appropriate MRI advisors. An RFP allows board members to set priorities, clearly define their areas of interest, and determine exactly how they want to enter this market. *(See Appendix 2 for Request for Proposal for Mission-Related Investment Financial Consultant.)*

Traditional foundation career paths have not developed people with the necessary combination of program and investment skills needed for mission-related investing. Program officers, who have come largely from the academic or nonprofit world, have grown up professionally separate from the more finance-oriented investment staff. This separation is exacerbated by the general sense that a foundation's core activity is grantmaking to nonprofits while investment remains a financially-driven staff function supported by external investment managers. Smaller foundations may be able to build teams with the appropriate mix of financial and program skills more readily than larger institutions.

The Investment Policy Statement

The investment policy statement is the central governing document which drives your mission-related investment strategy. It is the mission statement for your investments and concretely links your financial resources to your philanthropic purpose. Investment policy statements have clearly defined formats and typically include the following:

Statement of Objectives

The statement of objectives ties the investment policy to the mission and goals of the foundation. This section may include language which outlines your foundation's philosophy of investment. For example, The Jessie Smith Noyes Foundation's Investment Policy states:

"We recognize that our fiduciary responsibility does not end with maximizing return and minimizing risk. We also recognize that economic growth can come at considerable cost to communities and the environment. We believe that efforts to mitigate environmental degradation, address issues of social justice and promote healthy communities should be incorporated as part of business and investment decision making. We believe that management, directors, employees and investors should consider these social issues in the pursuit of financial objectives.

We believe that in light of the social, environmental and economic challenges of our time, fiduciary responsibility in the coming decades will dictate the integration of prudent financial management practices with principles of environmental stewardship, concern for community, and corporate accountability to shareholders and stakeholders alike. We believe that foundations have a particular role to play in this process, seeing their mission not only in terms of the uses of income to fund programs, but also in terms of the ends toward which endowment assets are managed. We believe that it is essential to reduce the dissonance between philanthropic mission and endowment management."[11]

Spending Goals

The spending policy establishes a financial timeframe for your foundation. Do you intend the foundation to last in perpetuity or should it operate for some targeted period of years? While this decision is driven by your program objectives, it will profoundly affect the investment strategies applied to your endowment.

Payout Policy

All U.S. foundations must payout at least 5% of their net assets as qualifying distributions. These qualifying distributions include grants and administrative and programmatic expenses related to grantmaking. Those mission-related investments which are classified as program-related investments are considered part of the payout requirement. Investment expenses cannot be included in the payout.

Asset Allocation

Once you have established a spending and payout strategy, the board will need to calculate the return requirement and, most importantly, develop an asset allocation strategy which reflects the foundation's risk tolerance and investment time horizon. This should outline the acceptable range for each asset class as a percentage of the overall portfolio. You should also address the rebalancing procedures to be used at least annually when the actual asset allocation deviates from the target allocation. Appropriate performance benchmarks need to be established for each asset class to determine your relative rate of return and evaluate the performance of your money managers.

Proxy Voting Guidelines

As equity shareholders in public companies, your foundation has the right to vote on various governance matters such as the election of the board of directors and on various resolutions which require shareholder approval. Shares held through mutual funds are not able to be voted, although the mutual fund managers must disclose how they have voted. Most foundations delegate the responsibility for proxy voting to individual investment managers. The policy may simply state that the investment committee will vote proxies in the best interest of the foundation and its mission or may be more specific in detailing which issues are important to the foundation.

Policy Oversight and Monitoring

The Investment Policy Statement should also outline the responsibilities for various investment-related tasks, e.g. board investment committee, key staff person, outside investment consultants and managers.

---

7 Kinder, Peter, "The Virtue of Consistency: The Gates Foundation & Mission-Related Investing," 2007, pg. 3.

8 McGray, Douglas, "Network Philanthropy," The Los Angeles Times, January 21, 2007, and Omidyar Network's website: www.omidyar.net.

9 For discussions of the fiduciary and tax implications of mission-related investing, see Freshfields Bruckhaus Deringer, A Legal Framework for Integrating Environmental, Social and Governance Issues into Institutional Investment, London, 2005. The UNEP Finance Initiative commissioned this major study conducted by Freshfields Bruckhaus Deringer, a leading international law firm, of the law in several countries regarding the duty of public and private pension fiduciaries and whether there were legal impediments to the incorporation of environmental, social and governance issues into investment decisions. The conclusion was that under the modern prudent investor rule institutional decision-makers are given latitude to follow a wide range of diversified investment strategies, provided their choice of investments is rational and economically defensible. The rule recognizes that different investments play different roles within a balanced portfolio. Because there is no duty to maximize the return of individual investments, the prudence of any specific investment will only be assessed within the context of the overall investment strategy. Also see Johnson, Kyle, Social Investing, Appendix B, Cambridge Associates LLC, 2007 for a thorough description of the Uniform Prudent Management of Institutional Funds Act (UPMIFA) and the Uniform Management of Institutional Funds Act (UMIFA); Emerson, Jed and Tim Little, with Jonas Kron, The Prudent Trustee: The Evolution of the Long-Term Investor, Generation Foundation and the Rose Foundation for Communities and the Environment; and Social Investment Forum, The Mission in the Marketplace: How Responsible Investing Can Strengthen the Fiduciary Oversight of Foundation Endowments and Enhance Philanthropic Missions, 2007.

10 This section is drawn from Hagerman, Lisa A., Gordon L. Clark, and Tessa Hebb, Massachusetts Pension Reserves Investment Management Board: Urban Investing through a Transparent Selection Process, Labor & Worklife Program, Harvard Law School, August 2007. (The complete case study is available at: http://urban.ouce.ox.ac.uk/research.php.)

11 See Appendix 1 for The Jessie Smith Noyes Foundation's investment policy statement.

Chapter 3:

Expanding the Philanthropic Investment Toolbox

Risk, Return AND Impact

Your foundation's MRI implementation should be driven by your program impact goals in conjunction with your organization's risk tolerance and financial return objectives. Building on the language of traditional investment theory, your optimal portfolio is a function of not only risk and return, but also a third dimension: impact. It is important to note that there is not a linear relationship between impact and risk or return. For example, taking more risk does not mean you have a greater social impact. Conversely, giving up return will not automatically translate into greater impact.

"How does this mission-related investment opportunity affect our program objectives and how does it fit within our overall risk and return goals?"

Answering this question can be very useful in determining which MRI tools and tactics are right for your foundation. For example, The F.B. Heron Foundation developed a mission-related investment continuum to provide a framework within the foundation's overall asset allocation to

Mission-Related Investment Continuum

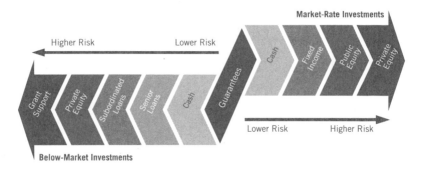

Source: The F.B. Heron Foundation

evaluate mission-related investment opportunities. By viewing grants as part of a broader range of philanthropic tools available to foundations to create impact, F.B. Heron has been able to seek out the best agents for achieving impact in a program area be they non-profit or for-profit. F.B. Heron has systematically built out its mission-related investment portfolio across a range of asset classes and program areas while increasing the total share of mission-related investments in its endowment to 25% and maintaining its total financial returns in the second quartile of its peer group.[12] This expansion followed a clear investment discipline and conformed to the foundation's overall asset allocation policy, performance benchmarks and prudent underwriting practices.

Matching Program with Investment Opportunities

Some foundations will face the challenge of finding mission-appropriate market-rate and below-market investment opportunities. While a foundation focusing on community development will find a range of investment products targeting affordable housing, enterprise development and access to capital, other program areas may not have the breadth of readily available products. Regional programs may require customized products. Conversations with current grantees about their funding and capital needs may make you aware of mission-related investment opportunities. In general, capital intensive areas such as housing are easier candidates for mission-related investing than human service organizations. A recent study by FSG Social Impact Advisors found that 85% of all mission-investment dollars invested between 2001 and 2005 were focused on four program areas: economic development, housing, education, and the environment.[13] Foundations active in specific areas may need to build a platform of products relevant to their mission. Nevertheless, new product offerings are increasing with many new options across program areas. On the next page, you will see a sample of what MRI opportunities exist across some of the traditional issue areas for foundations.

Market-Rate & Below-Market Mission-Related Investments Across Program Areas

Foundation Program Area	Mission-Related Investment Product
Affordable Housing	• Certificates of Deposit with Community Development Financial Institutions • Habitat for Humanity's Linda Mae Bonds • New York City Acquisition Fund
Culture & Open Media	• Participant Productions (Skoll) • Public Radio Capital • TRF's Artists' Housing Financing Fund
Education	• Housing Partnership Network's Charter School Financing Partnership
Environment	• Clean Tech Venture Funds • Pico Bonito Fund • Sea Change Fund • SJF Venture Fund
Health	• Deutsche Bank Eye Fund • International Finance Facility for Immunization • PATH (Program for Appropriate Technology in Health) • PRI loans to Community Clinics
International	• Accion International • Actis Capital Private Equity • Calvert Social Investment Fund • Oasis Investment Fund
Sustainable Communities	• Bay Area Smart Growth Fund I & II • Green Building Fund I • Rose Smart Growth Fund
Women's Empowerment	• Deutsche Bank Microcredit Development Fund • Project Enterprise • Women-owned Businesses Funds • Women's World Banking

12 *For a case study of The F.B. Heron Foundation, see Southern New Hampshire University, School of Community Economic Development,* Expanding Philanthropy: Mission-Related Investing at The F.B. Heron Foundation, *2007. (www.fbheron.org)*

13 *See Cooch, Sarah and Mark Kramer,* Compounding Impact: Mission Investing by US Foundations, *FSG Social Impact Advisors, 2007, pg. 4.*

Chapter 4:

Concrete Tools and Tactics

Active Ownership Strategies	Screening	Below-Market Investments	Guarantees	Market-Rate Investments

Mission-related investment tools and tactics vary among foundations, but they typically consist of a combination of active ownership strategies, screening of securities, below-market investments, guarantees, and market-rate investments. Your specific tools and tactics will depend upon your portfolio structure, staff capacity, program objectives, and strategy.

1. Active Ownership Strategies

Active Ownership Strategies	Screening	Below-Market Investments	Guarantees	Market-Rate Investments

As long-term owners and fiduciaries, foundations have the ability to influence corporate behavior and further their own missions through proxy voting, shareholder resolutions and informal shareholder engagement with corporate management. Examples abound of foundation boards which fund organizations trying to address environmental and social issues in part caused by the activities of corporations held in the foundation's endowment portfolio. While the logic of "knowing what you own" and avoiding public companies which are at odds with program goals is very compelling, some foundations question the impact of these strategies to truly affect corporate behavior given the large scale and liquidity of the equity markets. Others see these active ownership strategies as effective, long-term tactics to create more transparency and better information about corporate behavior. Given that these strategies can be executed with relatively little incremental expense, selective shareholder engagement can be a good strategy for smaller organizations or as a low-cost first step in MRI.

Proxy Voting

The vast majority of foundations do not vote their proxies, with many boards unaware of the mechanics of proxy voting.[14] Proxy voting guidelines should be outlined in your investment policy statement. Your board may incorrectly assume that external investment managers with a broad mandate to act in the best interests of the foundation will vote accordingly. In fact, most investment managers cast proxies in support of company management. The Nathan Cummings Foundation has approved the following explicit proxy voting policy:

> *"The Foundation will exercise its rights as a shareholder to vote its proxies on proposals put forth by management and shareholders as follows:*

> *On matters of program interest — when a program interest is at stake, the Foundation will vote in line with the program interest.*

> *On matters of corporate governance — the Foundation will vote in line with the broader*

programmatic objectives of accountability,
transparency, incentives for appropriate institutional
reforms, possibilities for systemic solutions and
ethical concerns."[15]

Your board can provide specific guidelines to outside service providers to obtain background research and voting recommendations for each proxy vote. These include ISS Governance Services, a unit of Risk Metrics (www.issproxy.com/issgovernance.html), Proxy Governance, Inc. (www.proxygovernance.com/content/pgi/content/about.shtml), Swingvote (www.swingvote.com) and Glass Lewis (http://www.glasslewis.com/solutions/proxypaper.php.) If your endowment's investments are held in mutual funds, you will not be able to directly vote your proxies. However, the mutual fund managers must disclose to you how they voted the proxies of the shares in the mutual fund. You can also engage your fund managers in discussions about how they vote proxies or choose your fund based on its objectives and proxy policies.

You can also bring the decision-making and proxy voting directly to your board. Your organization may want to pick a particular issue where you can have a direct impact and where a campaign may be directly linked to the work of your grantees. In fact, some foundations send a list of their portfolio holdings and describe their resolutions to their grantees to find areas of joint interest and action.

Shareholder Resolutions

Resolutions are shareholder proposals which are voted on at the corporation's annual meeting and may require management to follow or refrain from an identified policy. These resolutions cannot deal with the day-to-day management practices of the

Educational Foundation of America's (EFA) Old Growth Timber Campaign

The Educational Foundation of America (www.efaw.org) supports programs predominantly in the environment, population, Native American issues, and civic engagement. Its mission is to leverage social change through grants as well as through positive and negative screening of its investments, shareholder campaigns, proxy voting, and program-related investments. Founded in 1959, the $200 million foundation began with negative screening in 1994, and has since expanded into shareholder activism and positive screening with investments in clean tech and alternative energy funds. John Powers, a board and finance committee member of EFA, emphasizes the value of comparative quantitative performance data of screened vs. unscreened portfolios even though philanthropists may start with mission-related investing for qualitative ethical reasons. Much like the builders of environmental management systems, EFA combines screening and shareholder advocacy with grants to address root causes of social and environmental problems rather than supporting adaptation to problems with "tailpipe solutions."

In 1999, Home Depot announced that it would phase out the sale of old growth timber in its stores, but then was slow to implement the policy. EFA was the lead filer of the shareholder initiative, guided by the As You Sow Foundation. As You Sow engaged with Home Depot until the sales ended in 2003. Home Depot needed to work with its suppliers such as Boise-Cascade in order to meet the No Old Growth Timber goal. At the same time, EFA was supporting environmental NGOs, such as the Rainforest Action Network, which were also working on the Old Growth Timber Campaign. This inside/outside approach of shareholder and NGO engagement moved the campaign to successful results.

operation of the business. Shareholders typically begin a dialogue with a targeted company by requesting a change in the corporation's actions. If the company does not respond, a formal resolution may be filed as the next step.

Shareholder Coalitions

Given that the rules for shareholder resolutions are defined by the Security and Exchange Commission (SEC), which requires a minimum number of votes to include a resolution in the proxy, it can make sense for foundations to join shareholder coalitions for greater impact. Some of these coalitions have grown out of specific issues such as climate change (Coalition for Environmentally Responsible Economies — www.ceres.org) while others are umbrella organizations which track a wide range of issues and can provide information on emerging issues as well as coordinating support for ongoing shareholder resolutions. These shareholder coalitions include:

United Nations Principles for Responsible Investment (www.unpri.org)

The UN PRI provides investors with a framework for giving appropriate consideration to environmental, social, and governance (ESG) issues that can affect the performance of their investment portfolios. UN PRI signatories include asset owners and managers with over $10 trillion in assets under management.

Interfaith Center on Corporate Responsibility (www.iccr.org)

ICCR is a 35 year old international coalition of 275 faith-based institutional investors including denominations, religious communities, pension funds, healthcare corporations, foundations, and dioceses with combined portfolios of approximately $110 billion. ICCR members sponsor over 200 shareholder resolutions each year on social and environmental issues.

Carbon Disclosure Project (www.cdproject.net)
CDP coordinates institutional investors with a combined $41 trillion of assets under management. Its goal is to create a lasting relationship between shareholders and corporations regarding the implications for shareholder value and commercial operations presented by climate change.

2. Screening

Active Ownership Strategies	Screening	Below-Market Investments	Guarantees	Market-Rate Investments

Screening is the practice of buying and selling publicly-traded securities based on an evaluation of non-financial return criteria that reflect your foundation's mission. Your investment decision may be to avoid certain companies (negative screening) or to support particular companies (positive or best-in-class screening). The goal is for your portfolio to reflect the values of your organization, guard your reputation, mitigate risks, and use your investment capital to encourage or discourage specific corporate behaviors. An MRI consultant can work with your board to develop an appropriate screening strategy and to determine particular industries to avoid or to support while working to achieve your overall investment goals. Social screening supplements a range of other investment selection criteria such as financial performance and price-to-earnings ratios, management quality, and market capitalization.

Screening Methods and Strategies

Social screening research providers can customize the screens applied to your portfolio, or your organization may decide to buy socially-screened mutual funds. A screened fund which excludes entire industries such as nuclear power or weapons manufacturing or tobacco will not track the underlying unscreened benchmark; however, many best-in-class screened funds, which do not exclude industries, seek to outperform the unscreened benchmarks. Investment managers may propose appropriate substitute investments for those which have been screened from your portfolio. An inherent challenge is that large companies are often engaged in many areas. A company may produce equipment for nuclear power and for solar power, which can put investors in a bind between a negative and a positive screen that could advocate both for and against the same company at a given moment in time. Investors may also choose to divest of the stock of companies that are active in particular regions, e.g. South Africa during apartheid, or have particular practices, e.g. predatory lending or exploitation of child labor. A screened index fund can be a low-cost option if the fund's screening approach is in alignment with your mission.

Some positively-screened funds which target specific sectors such as renewable energy, environmental technology, or microfinance may have more risk due to their undiversified sector risk or the early stage ventures in their portfolios. These funds should not be benchmarked against index funds, and each fund will have a distinct investment strategy. For example, in 2004, Vice President Al Gore, joined with David Blood, formerly of Goldman Sachs Asset Management to launch Generation Asset Management, an institutional investment management firm dedicated to investing for sustainability by incorporating social, economic, environmental and ethical

Case Study
The Boston Foundation's Two-Tiered Sudan Screening

The Boston Foundation (TBF), (www.tbf.org), with assets of more than $800 million, has a long history of mission-related investing going back to the South African divestment campaign in the 1980s. TBF was also the first community foundation in the U.S. to vote its proxies. TBF's Socially Responsible Investment Policy focuses on four areas: corporate governance, environmental stewardship, community well-being and stewardship, and diversity and equity.

In March 2007, The Boston Foundation decided to distance itself from companies that are engaged in business with the government of Sudan, which has been financing military conflicts in the Darfur region of the country with its oil revenues. TBF's two-part screening strategy consists of the divestment of any direct holdings of companies operating in Sudan and a new approach of shorting stocks which are held indirectly by the foundation in pooled funds. "Using our assets to move an ethical agenda forward is an important part of the history and culture of The Boston Foundation," said Paul S. Grogan, President and CEO.

factors into their assessment of global large-cap corporations.[16] Generation Asset Management is one of several investment firms which position themselves, not as positively screened funds, but rather as long-term investors which consider sustainability as part of fundamental financial analysis.

MARKET-RATE OR BELOW-MARKET?

You should be clear at the beginning of your review whether a mission-related investment opportunity is market-rate or below-market. Some opportunities may arrive seeking below-market funding but which could support market-rate, or vice versa. Below-market transactions should be below-market not because the venture seeks less expensive funding, or because below-market funding makes the donor feel better, but rather because the below-market funding addresses a critical funding gap, leverages additional capital, and delivers social impact. As one foundation CFO said, "Blended value can often be the refuge for underperformance." Below-market funding and grants are the scarcest resources in the mission-related investment capital market and should be used only when they can create incremental social impact.

The F.B. Heron Foundation has quantified the opportunity cost due to below-market pricing at 30-50 basis points of its overall portfolio return. They believe that this cost is justified given the fact that $1 of below-market funding from Heron will typically leverage $12 of capital from other sources. In addition, the below-market portfolio has very low volatility due to its lower correlation to market-rate investments.

3. Below-Market Investments

Active Ownership Strategies	Screening	Below-Market Investments	Guarantees	Market-Rate Investments

Program-Related Investments (PRIs)

Below-market investments made by foundations are typically categorized as program-related investments (PRIs). As mentioned in the earlier section on fiduciary duty, PRIs[17] are defined by the U.S. tax code as investments made by foundations in support of their charitable purposes and without an expectation of a commercial return, adjusted for risk and mission. The code states that a PRI is not explicitly required to earn below-market returns, but rather a PRI cannot be structured to maximize returns. However, if a PRI such as a successful equity investment exceeds its expected return, its status as a PRI is not changed. A PRI also counts toward your foundation's pay-out requirement.

PRIs can serve various purposes, such as making a non-profit organization more "investment-ready" by promoting financial sustainability and better management. In financial management terms, a PRI requires an organization to focus on using its balance sheet as well as its income statement. A PRI also sends a positive signal to other potential funders and investors.

Although the majority of PRIs made by foundations have been loans, opportunities exist in a range of asset classes such as commodities, e.g. sustainable lumber, real estate, and private equity funds. Foundations making PRIs must build the systems and processes to track interest, repayments, equity exits, and program covenants. As a beginning PRI maker, you may want to co-invest with more experienced PRI makers, or make PRIs through intermediaries instead of making direct PRIs. You may also want to utilize third-party due diligence to increase the quality of your underwriting process.

Case Study

Packard PRI Loan Launches Sustainable Seafood Private Equity Fund

The David and Lucile Packard Foundation (www.packard.org) has long been working to restore health to the world's endangered oceans, both through grants and program-related investments. A study by the Food and Agricultural Organization of the United Nations found that 60% of the world's important fish stocks are "in urgent need of management" to rehabilitate them or keep them from being overfished. Nevertheless, as consumers, we receive little information about the seafood we buy. Although there is growing consumer demand for sustainable seafood products, the missing link in the supply chain is at the distribution level between the fishermen and consumers. "We found that while there were fishermen who would go out and fish sustainably, the distributors would just dump it all in with what a trawler caught, decimating the seas," said Curt Riffle, program operations manager at Packard.

The Sea Change Investment Fund (www.seachangefund.com) was launched in 2005 to address this gap in the market. Packard saw that it could not achieve its program goal of altering market behavior solely through grants. Sea Change has total assets of $20 million with half coming from a PRI loan from Packard and the other half from private investors. Packard made its $10 million loan to encourage other investors. "We also used the Packard Foundation's commitment to go out to the investors, to convince them we were serious. We didn't want a grant to do this, because we didn't want to say that we've been capitalized on the basis of a gift or giveaway that we're not accountable for," said Jason Winship, Managing Principal at Sea Change. The PRI loan will be repaid from fund proceeds prior to any distributions to the other investors.

Any company under review for a Sea Change investment undergoes a two-level process. A nine-member conservation committee, staffed by leaders in conservation and fishery science, determines if the potential investment meets the sustainability criteria. If the conservation committee does approve, the investment candidate moves on to an investment committee with four members from commercial and financial backgrounds similar to those of traditional venture capital firms. To date, Sea Change has made early stage equity investments in four companies. The companies must agree to explicit environmental covenants regarding their ongoing operations. Sea Change's double-bottom line approach hopes to deliver results by making sustainable seafood mainstream.

4. Guarantees

Active Ownership Strategies	Screening	Below-Market Investments	Guarantees	Market-Rate Investments

Guarantees and other non-cash structures can be attractive alternatives to cash loans when providing debt capital in a mission-related investment. Guarantees separate the credit risk of an organization from the funding of a loan to that organization. A foundation typically uses its endowment as collateral to provide security (guarantee) to an intermediary which then funds the organization based on this security. The IRS does not treat guarantees as part of a foundation's payout. However, some foundations use linked deposits with depository institutions such as community development financial institutions (CDFIs) in order to count the PRI as a part of their payout. In a linked deposit, the foundation makes a deposit with the CDFI, and the CDFI agrees to make a loan to an organization secured by or "linked to" that deposit. Guarantees from foundations and individuals have also been used by organizations such as Micro Credit Enterprises (www.mcenterprises.org) to secure lines of credit to make loans to international microfinance institutions which, in turn, provide small loans to poor entrepreneurs.

Guarantees can enhance an organization's access to capital by lowering the risk to its market-rate lenders and by connecting organizations to capital markets. Guarantees are part of a range of creative options which a foundation can use in structuring a mission-related investment. For example, your foundation can give a grant to an organization in order to "buy down" the interest rate or cover the closing costs of a loan from a bank. This achieves your goal of funding the organization on favorable terms, but does not require your foundation to monitor and service a loan.

Robin Hood Leverages Common Ground's Supportive Housing Mission

Robin Hood (www.robinhood.org), a New York City-based foundation, works to fight poverty in the city by applying investment principles to philanthropy. As part of its Survival program area, Robin Hood supports Common Ground's (www.commonground.org) work to solve homelessness through preventive programs and through initiatives that place homeless people directly in permanent housing. In Common Ground's supportive housing, formerly homeless people, many of whom have mental illness or AIDS, live in settings that provide social services on site such as mental health and substance abuse counseling, and job training. Common Ground has developed and currently manages seven buildings that house over 1,700 people in permanent and temporary residences.

Common Ground's goal is to build 4,000 additional units of supportive housing in New York City by 2015. However, Common Ground has been unable to compete with private developers for development sites to build supportive housing in New York's booming real estate market. Although there was sufficient long-term permanent public sector financing for Common Ground, the organization did not have the flexible, early stage capital it needed to acquire a site and cover its "soft" costs, that is for design and professional consulting fees, not for tangible materials. To address this capital gap, Common Ground worked with a group of philanthropic and private sector investors to structure a $10 million pre-development and acquisition fund consisting of $2 million of higher-risk, subordinated debt from philanthropic investors and $8 million of senior commercial financing. The senior commercial lenders looked to the philanthropic capital as security for their loans. Robin Hood structured its participation in the $2 million philanthropic loan as a guarantee in the form of a stand-by letter of credit. Through this guarantee structure, Robin Hood was able to support Common Ground's expansion without using its scarce grant resources.

5. Market-Rate Investments

Active Ownership Strategies	Screening	Below-Market Investments	Guarantees	Market-Rate Investments

Foundations which invest in market-rate transactions will find opportunities to co-invest with a broad range of institutional investors such as CalPERS and MassPRIM which seek to earn a risk-adjusted market rate of return in addition to creating environmental, social and governance benefits. These institutional investors are not philanthropies and therefore are not permitted to make below-market investments.

Many investments will target specific geographic regions or countries, and the investment managers may partner with local nonprofits in order to achieve and evaluate specific social outcomes. Although the active ownership and screening strategies outlined earlier also address "market-rate" investments, we are focusing in this section on investment opportunities which direct capital to organizations or projects which create specific social outcomes. These include examples such as regional smart-growth bond funds, urban private equity funds, and certificates of deposit placed with community development financial institutions. There has been a significant increase in mission-related private equity funds particularly in the areas of clean tech, community development, and funds which actively target women- and minority-owned businesses. Mission-related real estate investment opportunities have grown along with the interest in transit-friendly development, brownfield redevelopment, workforce housing, and green buildings.[18] In the fixed income asset class, your foundation can also find separately managed municipal bonds, mortgage-backed securities and asset-backed securities which can be customized to your program area and targeted geographic regions. Mutual fund products are also available.

Sheep in Wolf's Clothing?

Mission-related investors need to assess the social impact of potential investments as part of their due diligence process. Some market-rate mission-related investments may not appear with a "social investing" label, despite having significant environmental and social benefits. As a foundation CFO

Case Study
Kalamazoo Community Foundation's Local Venture Investments

The Kalamazoo Community Foundation (www.kalfound.org), with approximately $260 million in assets, actively supports local economic development. In 2000, the foundation's board authorized $13 million for program-related investments and $5 million for locally-targeted venture capital.

The foundation has since partnered with Southwest Michigan First, Kalamazoo County's economic development corporation, to provide a $2 million program-related investment to complete the financing of an Innovation Center in the Business Technology Research Park of Western Michigan University. The center supports scientists previously employed by the Pharmacia/Upjohn pharmaceutical company (now Pfizer), who are beginning their own early-stage biotech and life sciences companies. This $12 million facility is already home to 14 small businesses.

On the venture capital side, the foundation has invested as a limited partner in three funds totaling $3 million. The foundation seeks firms with significant ownership or venture capital presence in the Kalamazoo community.[19]

recently observed, "our investment manager brought in a private equity timber deal, and we found that it really was a sustainable forestry investment." The opposite can also be true. A fund may move away from its stated social mission as it adds portfolio companies. A community revitalization fund can easily become a vehicle for displacement and gentrification. It is best to negotiate clear program outputs and reporting requirements prior to making your investment in order to increase the likelihood that your desired social impacts will be achieved.

14 *Rockefeller Philanthropy Advisors and As You Sow Foundation,* Unlocking the Power of the Proxy, *2003; and Lipman, Harvey, "Meshing Proxy with Mission: Few Foundations Do Much to Influence Shareholder Votes,"* Chronicle of Philanthropy, *May 4, 2006.*

15 *See http://www.nathancummings.org/news/Policy_Statement_2002.pdf.*

16 *Mendonca, Lenny T. and Jeremy Oppenheim, "Investing in Sustainability: An Interview with Al Gore and David Blood,"* The McKinsey Quarterly, *May 2007.*

17 *For more information on PRI-specific strategies, see* Program-Related Investing: Skills & Strategies for New PRI Funders, *Grantcraft, 2006.*

18 *For an extensive survey of market-rate mission-related investments within specific asset classes, see Wood, David and Belinda Hoff,* Handbook on Responsible Investment Across Asset Classes, *The Institute of Responsible Investing at the Boston College Center for Corporate Citizenship, 2007. Also see William M. Dietel,* Mission Stewardship: Aligning Programs, Investments, and Administration to Achieve Impact, *The F.B. Heron Foundation, 2007.*

19 *See* Kalamazoo Gazette, *October 11, 2007.*

Chapter 5:

Building the Pipeline: Execution Matters

Finding Investment Opportunities

After addressing the key strategic, governance, investment and product considerations of mission-related investment, trustees and your organization's staff still face the challenge of finding transactions, executing them, and successfully generating social impact. Your success will depend on your search efforts, the ability to tap internal and external resources, and the building of a network of relationships. As with your grantmaking activities, waiting for investment proposals will result in a very different universe of opportunities than if you are actively building a pipeline of deals based on your program goals.

While many foundation boards can rely on outside investment consultants and investment advisors to find traditional market-rate transactions, these outsourcing options may not be readily available for mission-related investment. Many segments of this market operate on a brokered, merchant-banking model where organizations raise capital by negotiating specific terms and conditions with each investor. Placement agents are active in some of the larger, market-rate sectors such as affordable housing. Nevertheless, the mission-related investment market infrastructure is still under construction with an ongoing need for more market makers, new financial

MISSION-RELATED INVESTMENT MARKET RESOURCES

While websites, conferences, and databases are great sources of information to better understand the mission-related market landscape and players, there is no substitute for actively building a pipeline of deals by talking to other investors, intermediaries, and capital-raising organizations active in your program area. These may include non-foundation investors such as banks, insurance companies, pension funds and endowments. A wide range of organizations offer sector-specific information on mission-related investing. They include:

- Blended Value (www.blendedvalue.org);
- CleanTech Venture Network (www.cleantechnetwork.com);
- Community Development Bankers Association (www.communitydevelopmentbanks.org);
- Community Development Venture Capital Alliance (www.cdvca.org);
- Community Investing Center Database (www.communityinvestingcenterdb.org);
- Initiative for a Competitive Inner City (www.icic.org);
- Investors Circle (www.investorscircle.net);
- MIX Market Microfinance Information Platform (www.mixmarket.org);
- PRI Makers Network (www.primakers.net);
- Research Initiative on Social Entrepreneurship (www.riseproject.org);
- Social Investment Forum (www.socialinvest.org);
- Social Venture Network (www.svn.org);
- The UNEP Finance Initiative Asset Management Working Group (www.unepfi.org/work_streams/investment); and
- Xigi.net (www.xigi.net)

instruments, and consistent benchmarks. Supply and demand need to co-evolve.

It is important to note that the dynamic between investors and the capital-raisers has much more "give and take" than traditional donor-grantee relationships. Co-investors may include a broad range of institutional investors such as insurance companies, banks, pension funds, endowments and individuals. As a mission-related investor, you will have to respond to opportunities and negotiate terms. The public sector may also participate directly as a co-investor or indirectly by providing credit enhancement or refinancing of specific transactions.

Wholesale or Retail? Investing through Intermediaries

Your foundation will need to decide how to allocate its MRI portfolio between direct investments and investments made through intermediaries. Intermediaries can range from small community-based loan funds to global mutual fund companies. In its recent report on intermediaries, FSG Social Impact Advisors defined a mission investment intermediary as "an entity that accepts investment funds and re-invests them in other organizations in order to achieve social impact and some level of financial return for its investors. Intermediaries typically focus on one issue area (e.g., affordable housing, the environment, economic development) and build specialized portfolios of investee organizations addressing that issue. By placing capital in an investment intermediary, a foundation can impact multiple organizations within the portfolio."[20]

By making direct investments, a foundation can negotiate specific terms and conditions. By using an intermediary, you can potentially leverage other funders and execute transactions more efficiently and at a larger scale. For many foundations with limited staff, mission investing intermediaries provide access to investment opportunities which would not be available as direct investments. Foundations, which target direct service providers for their grantmaking, may see intermediaries as costly middlemen, who use resources which could be better placed through direct investments. However, depending on your specific program objectives, you may be able to leverage very effectively the expertise and scope of intermediaries. In certain program areas which may not have highly evolved intermediaries, some foundations are actively working to build appropriate intermediaries. Asset allocation objectives and portfolio risk tolerance should also be considered when evaluating the use of intermediaries.

Due Diligence

As the first step in the due diligence process, your staff will typically prepare a brief note on the opportunity to the board investment committee. At this point, both financial and program staff will have an opportunity to raise specific issues. This is not a pre-approval but a way to efficiently direct staff resources toward closeable deals. This step also permits the board and foundation management to be sure that specific questions which they have about the organization and transaction will be addressed in the formal due diligence process. Some foundations establish requirements such as having a grant relationship with an organization before making a MRI to that organization. Investors can delegate or centralize the decision-making process

Intermediaries and Innovation: The New Hampshire Community Loan Fund's Resident Owned Communities Program

The New Hampshire Community Loan Fund (www.theloanfund.org) provided loans of almost $18 million to low- and moderate-income families in 2006. Founded in 1983, the Fund provides financial, human and civic resources to enable traditionally undeserved people to participate fully in New Hampshire's economy. The Fund is supported by grants as well as by loans from mission-related investors. These lenders can choose an interest rate of 0% to 4% for loans of four years or longer, or 0% to 3% for loans of one to three years.

The Fund supports a range of innovative projects including microlending, childcare facilities, homeownership and individual development accounts. Under its Manufactured Housing Park program, the Fund has made loans totaling $47 million, preserving 4,570 homes in 87 resident-owned communities (ROCs), and leveraging financing of $130 million through 2007. Unlike other homeowners, owners of manufactured or "mobile" homes in manufactured home communities ("MHC") have little opportunity to build equity in their homes and can even face eviction if the owner sells the property for redevelopment. A recent study[21] of the Fund's program found that residents who own their MHC can realize higher average home sales prices, faster home sales, and greater access to fixed rate home financing than homeowners who do not own the community in which their homes are sited.

In the second ROC conversion in 1985, the Fund provided a bridge loan to the Souhegan Valley Manufactured Housing Cooperative until the community could get a $350,000 Community Development Block Grant to acquire their community and avoid imminent displacement due to the landlord's proposed change of land use. Through its twenty years of ownership, the residents have been able to upgrade the community's infrastructure while keeping site fees

continued

low. "My proudest accomplishment is helping us become a co-op and buying the park, because it's something people said we couldn't do," said Florence Quast, a resident of Souhegan Valley. By 2006, more than 17% of the manufactured housing parks in New Hampshire had been converted to ROCs. Banks are now recognizing the ROC market segment and providing more favorable mortgage financing to both the cooperatives for purchasing the community and now directly to homeowners and homebuyers for home loans. Given that 3.5 million American families reside in over 50,000 MHC, the Fund has joined several national partners to launch ROC USA with the goal of building the infrastructure to support homeowners in seizing the opportunity that home and land ownership represents.

depending on their size and culture. Decision-making about market-rate mission-related investments should reflect the same level of analysis as other endowment investments with additional analysis of the program aspects of the investment. The initial transactions may require a higher level of scrutiny until your staff and board develop comfortable working relationships with one another.

Threshold questions and issues to be addressed at this stage of due diligence include:

- How does this investment further specific program goals of our foundation?
- Will this investment enable a project to happen that otherwise would not?
- Could the program goals be better achieved with a grant?
- Is this a market-rate or below-market investment?
- Who are the principals involved in the investment?
- Does the transaction leverage other sources of capital?
- What are the program and financial risks and how are they distributed?

- Does the investment raise reputation or policy issues for the foundation?
- What is the source of repayment?
- Where would this transaction fit in our overall asset allocation?

Once the transaction has received a preliminary green light, the detailed due diligence review will begin. Basic documents to review at this point include multi-year, audited financial statements of the organization, other relevant organizational materials as well as project-specific documentation such as projections and business plans. For some organizations, it is possible to purchase "off-the-shelf" financial analysis from third party providers. More structured investments such as project financings, loan funds or investment in private equity funds will require a more customized financial analysis. A clear assessment of the quality of the management team and its commitment to program covenants in addition to the financial targets is a key part of the due diligence. When investing in an intermediary, it is necessary to assess the fund manager's ability to find portfolio companies and projects which will fit your program and investment goals. You may look to a fund manager's previous track record with placing and exiting investments as a good indicator of future success. Some foundations supplement internal, staff-driven due diligence with independent assessments from professional consultants.

The Investment Decision

The document created through the formal due diligence process will be an investment memorandum outlining the transaction

The KL Felicitas Foundation's Due Diligence Toolkit

The KL Felicitas Foundation (www.klfelicitasfoundation.org), a California-based family foundation, was established by the Kleissner family in 2000. The foundation's mission is to:

• Enable social entrepreneurs worldwide to develop and grow economically sustainable, scalable enterprises with high measurable social impact;

• Empower rural communities and families through sustainable economic and social change; and

• Advocate our foundation's leveraged mission, program and sustainability investment strategy.

To supplement their program activities, the Kleissners have developed a sustainability, mission, and social investment (SMSI) strategy. In their work with social entrepreneurs, they found a funding gap between grants and commercial finance. These SMSI investments are an overlay to their total asset allocation rather than a separate asset class. They target financial returns approximating the average risk-adjusted returns of similar investments made without regard to social, mission, or sustainable considerations. The only exception is program-related investment which can be up to 5% below the expected risk-adjusted return.

The Kleissners seek to ultimately incorporate most of their assets into the SMSI framework, not just their philanthropic entities. In conjunction with their advisors, the foundation has developed a series of MRI and PRI worksheets including due diligence and documentation checklists, and financial analysis templates which are included in Appendix 3 and are also available at www.klfelicitasfoundation.org.

Additional templates for Mission-Related Investment Due Diligence are available to members of the PRI Makers Network at www.primakers.net.

and providing a concise analysis of its potential opportunities and risks. This document will serve as the basis for the formal approval of the transaction within your foundation. The specific format will depend on the needs and decision-making processes in the foundation. Based on a review of the investment summaries of several foundations, the report may include sections such as:

- Investment Overview;
- Recommendation;
- Organizational Analysis;
- Management Quality;
- Transaction Risk Analysis; and
- Investment Rating.

MRI Scoring and Ratings

A mission-related investment scoring system can serve as a highly effective tool in assessing risk and distilling key issues into scores which can be used to compare investment opportunities. In order to better manage their portfolios, some foundations develop parallel ratings for Program Impact and Financial Risk/Returns in order to clearly assess both aspects of the transaction and incorporate the views of program and investment staff into your organization's overall rating for the investment opportunity. Based on this analysis, the foundation program and investment staff score the program and investment risks and construct an aggregate risk score for the investment opportunity. Market-rate investments will typically include more financial indicators and metrics than PRIs. The most useful scoring and ratings systems are those which are not overly formulaic and trigger an open conversation among the board, program and investment staff of the qualitative as well as quantitative merits of particular MRI opportunities. See Appendix 4 for a sample MRI Scoring Questionnaire. This same rating system can be revisited as part of your portfolio monitoring.

Risk Management

Due diligence may raise risk considerations which will require you to adjust the proposed structure. Many risk management practices such as standardizing documentation, co-investing, syndications, and using intermediaries can also lower execution costs and make mission-related transactions more efficient. Be careful not to create complex structures which do not address the underlying needs of the investees or may prove to be of no value when needed. For example, your foundation's willingness to foreclose on the building loan of a non-profit in default may be limited given reputation risk and program considerations. Intangible considerations such as management quality cannot be so easily addressed through financial structuring. However, financial and program covenants can provide you with the ability to bring the organization to the table to work through difficult issues. Some of the risk management expertise of your traditional investment advisors can be applied to your mission-related portfolio.

Risk management structures include:
- Setting specific performance hurdles as a condition to additional funding;
- Co-investing and participating in syndications of transactions underwritten by other investors;

- Taking collateral or seeking recourse to other creditworthy entities as a means of mitigating the risk of your investment;
- Limiting your investment to a particular project financing with its own source of repayment;
- Taking a senior or junior (subordinated) position in a particular structure in order to manage your risk or to attract additional third-party capital;
- Requiring the organization to demonstrate other sources of third party capital;
- Limiting your share of a total project to a percentage;
- Taking a seat or observer rights on the board or investor advisory committee; and
- Providing capacity-building grants to prepare a non-profit organization for a PRI.

Documentation and Closing

Although the desire to close a deal as quickly as possible is understandable, the process of translating the agreed terms and conditions of a mission-related investment into a series of enforceable legal documents can raise new issues. Mission-related investing is more document-intensive than grantmaking. You will need to balance the desire to use your standard documents as templates against the need to create customized legal documents which reflect the complexity of a specific transaction. The fact that many nonprofits rely on pro bono legal services in order to save expenses may also increase the time needed to close a transaction. You may want to set an expiration date on your funding commitment in order to create urgency with the investee to close as soon as possible. This transition from negotiation to documentation needs to be

Case Study

Packard's Credit Enhancement of LIIF's Initiative for Childcare in California

The Low Income Investment Fund (LIIF) (www.liifund.org) provides affordable capital and technical assistance to organizations working to alleviate poverty in low income neighborhoods. LIIF manages the Affordable Building for Children's Development (ABCD) Initiative — a statewide effort in California to provide finance, technical assistance, construction advice and advocacy to the underfunded preschool childcare sector.

The David and Lucile Packard Foundation (www.packard.org) has committed $14.5 million in grants and PRIs to LIIF for ABCD. This includes a $1 million Packard PRI which LIIF was able to leverage with $10 million in private sector capital from Impact Community Capital (www.impactcapital.net), a consortium of insurance companies using the New Markets Tax Credits program. The Impact Community Capital investors bear some governmental appropriations risk since the childcare facilities receive public operating support as well as refinancing risk from the partially amortizing loans to the facilities. However, Packard provided an innovative credit enhancement to the private investors to cover a portion of any losses on the pool of loans to the childcare facilities. The ABCD initiative leverages significant public funding as well.

Developers of new buildings are now coming to LIIF for its expertise in incorporating childcare facilities into their plans. LIIF would like to use the ABCD Initiative as a model for other states seeking to build sound financing models for childcare facilities. The ABCD Fund has committed 16 loans totaling $6.9 million and 20 planning grants. This financing will support over 2,700 quality childcare spaces. In total, the ABCD Fund hopes to assemble $30 to $40 million in a combination of private capital and philanthropic investments to finance up to 10,000 childcare spaces in California.

managed efficiently. In particular, the business people need to finalize terms and then work with legal counsel to generate documentation. Transactions which involve multiple investors can also require additional time and expense.

Portfolio Monitoring

Portfolio monitoring is a key part of risk management. By closely monitoring your mission-related investment portfolio, you can incorporate the lessons learned through your investments and limit losses or correct problems with an investment before losses are incurred. In fact, a recent report[22] by FSG Social Impact Advisors found that foundations, which track and monitor their mission-related investments, have much lower default rates. Monitoring and reporting cycles will depend on the complexity and risk of a particular asset class; however, most MRIs report their unaudited financials and covenant compliance on a quarterly basis with annual audited financial reports. It is necessary to communicate reporting expectations to an investee very clearly. If a foundation views its mission-related investment as an experiment and does not monitor its portfolio, the returns are typically lower. Certain investments require more intense monitoring than others. For example, a real estate project financing will be more demanding than a guaranteed certificate of deposit. Complex financial engineering and covenants are not meaningful if they are not tracked. The development and maintenance of a rating system with a watch list for riskier assets can also be very helpful.

20 *For analysis of intermediaries, see Cooch, Sarah and Mark Kramer,* Aggregating Impact: A Foundation's Guide to U.S. Mission Investment Intermediaries, *FSG Social Impact Advisors, Boston, 2007.*

21 *Ward, Sally K. Ph.D., Charlie French, Ph.D. and Kelly Giraud, Ph.D,* Building Value and Security for Homeowners in Mobile Home Parks: A Report on Economic Outcomes, *The Carsey Institute at the University of New Hampshire, 2006.*

22 *Cooch and Kramer,* Compounding Impact, *FSG Social Impact Advisors, Boston, pg. 25.*

Chapter 6:

Closing the Loop: Achieving Impact

By extending your philanthropy beyond grantmaking to include mission-related investing, you are seeking the best opportunities for achieving impact in a program area. With this goal in mind, how can you capture the impact of your activities and incorporate this knowledge to drive the future strategy and tactics of your foundation? The ultimate goal is to build a virtuous cycle of mission-driven capital, multiplying your impact and learning. However, foundations continue to face significant challenges in how to capture the impacts of their grantmaking let alone mission-related investments.

Defining Impact

In order to better understand how your mission-related investments are creating social and environmental impact, it is essential to be very clear about measurement. A key notion is to differentiate outputs from outcomes. Outputs are results that we can measure or assess directly. For example, outputs for a home-ownership program would include the number of housing units built or renovated. Outcomes are the ultimate changes that we are trying to make in the world. For the home-ownership program, an outcome might be increased wealth and quality of life for low-income people. It can sometimes be difficult to evaluate whether an outcome has been achieved. Nevertheless, an organization should define its desired outcomes and work to determine how the measurable outputs correlate to those outcomes. Impact is the next link in the chain. Impact is that portion of the total outcome which occurred as a result of the activity, above and beyond what would have happened anyway. For more information about social impact reporting, see the resources below as well as the Impact Value Chain developed as part of The Rockefeller Foundation's Double Bottom Line Project in Appendix 5.[23]

Financial & Social Performance Measurements

Social and environmental impacts are usually not comparable in the way that financial returns can be compared. Therefore, mission-related investors will track program-specific social metrics. For example, the Community Development Venture Capital Alliance (CDVCA) developed a Measuring Impacts Toolkit[24], which proposed the following community-development financial and social investment performance measures for CDVCA funds:

- Employment created or retained by low- to moderate-income employees;
- A measurement of wealth creation among target low- to moderate-income employees;
- Underlying job quality, e.g. benefits, training; and
- A measurement of economic development/public finance effects such as taxes generated.

Pension funds such as CalPERS have also developed metrics for their economically targeted investments which focus on "underserved markets." With the assistance of Pacific Community Ventures (www.pacificcommunityventures.org), CalPERS established the following performance objectives for its $475 million California Initiative:

• Financial Objective: Earn Risk-Adjusted Returns; and
• Non-Financial Objectives/Metrics:
  — Located in areas where institutional capital is limited;
  — Employ workers who reside in economically disadvantaged areas; and
  — Female/Minority management or ownership.

Pacific Community Ventures established some rules of thumb for non-financial reporting which can also apply to the mission-related investment activities of foundations: set expectations upfront, keep reporting requirements simple and be consistent, establish confidentiality policies about data, be realistic in measuring outputs and outcomes rather than measuring impacts, and incorporate your learning into your due diligence process for new transactions.

As mission-related investments are repaid or exited, the financial performance remains the easiest to capture and compare. Tracking the social impacts of an MRI investment beyond repayment or exit can be challenging as any program covenants and reporting requirements are no longer in effect. Many trustees may see this imperfect science of linking investment and social metrics as a reason to continue the strict separation of money from mission. We believe the opposite: by seeking to pull investment and social drivers together, you can better harness them both to achieve the ultimate goal of your philanthropy: impact.

23 *For more information about social impact reporting, see Clark, Catherine, William Rosenzweig, David Long, and Sara Olsen,* Double Bottom Line Project Report: Assessing Social Impact in Double Bottom Line Ventures, *The Rockefeller Foundation, 2004; and* Measuring Social Impact: The Foundation of Social Return on Investment, *London Business School and the New Economics Foundation.*

24 *www.cdvca.org*

Conclusion:

Engaging the New Passing Gear

We hope that this publication has informed you about the practice of mission-related investing. We believe that MRI can be an exciting and value-adding component of your foundation's mission and work. The process of creating an MRI policy and program at your foundation will be customized as no two foundations are the same. Nevertheless, we do see some common themes and principles:

- Mission-related investing is an extension of your philanthropy, not a substitute for it.

- Philanthropy and investment have much in common and will be more closely connected in the years to come.

- Mission-related investing by foundations is part of a larger institutional investor market including pension funds, endowments and banks.

- Program impact goals can and should drive your mission-related investment strategy.

- Create processes which are practical, disciplined and transparent.

- Build trust among board members, program and investment staff.

- Track and monitor your results — even if imperfectly.

- Reflect on and learn from your results; incorporate them in your ongoing strategy.

The temptation is to wait for a perfect system or process for MRI — it does not exist. What does exist is a body of work and programs that have been invented and developed by the pioneers in the growing community of MRI practitioners. That work is a strong platform upon which the rest of the philanthropic community can begin to construct its MRI programs.

Finally, MRI does not need to be an "all-or-nothing" proposition. You can start with a modest effort and go from there. The key idea is to begin and to learn.

The challenges facing our communities and the world are not going away and cannot wait for a perfect system of MRI. Philanthropy is needed more than ever before. We think it is time to engage the new passing gear of mission-related investing and accelerate philanthropy.

Appendix 1:

Jessie Smith Noyes Foundation Investment Policy

Statement of Fiduciary Responsibility

We recognize that our fiduciary responsibility does not end with maximizing return and minimizing risk. We also recognize that economic growth can come at considerable cost to communities and the environment. We believe that efforts to mitigate environmental degradation, address issues of social justice and promote healthy communities should be incorporated as part of business and investment decision making. We believe that management, directors, employees and investors should consider these social issues in the pursuit of financial objectives.

We believe that in light of the social, environmental and economic challenges of our time, fiduciary responsibility in the coming decades will dictate the integration of prudent financial management practices with principles of environmental stewardship, concern for community, and corporate accountability to shareholders and stakeholders alike.

We believe that foundations have a particular role to play in this process, seeing their mission not only in terms of the uses of income to fund programs, but also in terms of the ends toward which endowment assets are managed. We believe that it is essential to reduce the dissonance between philanthropic mission and endowment management.

Investment Philosophy

In concert with the Foundation's mission to protect and restore Earth's natural systems and promote a sustainable society by strengthening individuals, institutions and communities pledged to pursuing those goals, we seek, where possible, to invest our endowment assets in companies that:

- Provide commercial solutions to major social and environmental problems; and/or
- Build corporate cultures with concerns for environmental impact, equity and community.

The Foundation will look at:

- The environmental impact of a business by its use of materials, generation of waste, and the goods it produces or services it provides;
- Issues of equity within a corporation, particularly with regard to participatory management, employee ownership, salary structures, workforce diversity, employee benefit programs or other demonstrated commitments to the well-being of all individuals involved in an enterprise; and
- A corporation's openness and accountability to all stakeholders, its local job creation especially for the economically disadvantaged, its corporate giving to and active involvement with community organizations, or its other initiatives that provide net benefits to the local economy.

Spending & Investment Goals

The spending and investment goals of the foundation are:

- To generate income and capital gains necessary to support the foundation's operations and fund its grantmaking over the long-term;
- To provide capital directly to or own the equity or debt of enterprises which further the foundation's mission;
- To avoid investing in companies whose environmental or social impacts contribute to the issues that the foundation's grant-making seeks to address;
- To set spending levels based primarily on an assessment of current need and of current and projected investment returns; and
- To preserve, to the extent possible consistent with the foundation's spending levels, the real (inflation adjusted) value of its assets over the long term.

The Board of Directors has determined that the Foundation should be viewed as a perpetual institution. Therefore, investments that have the potential to generate substantial and long-term total returns that offset inflation will be important to pursue.

Investment Guidelines

Investment guidelines are based on a 20-year horizon. Interim performance will be monitored as appropriate.

Appreciation and income may be used to finance cash requirements for grants and operating expenses. Assets may be spent down during periods in which neither appreciation nor income is sufficient to fund grantmaking budgets.

The Foundation's assets will be managed by professional money managers that are selected by the Finance Committee. Assets are allocated in accordance with guidelines set forth by the Finance Committee and approved by the Board. Investment managers have discretion to manage the assets in each particular portfolio to best achieve investment objectives and requirements consistent with the social and financial guidelines set forth in the Foundation's Investment Policy. Managers will be monitored on a regular basis.

The managers are responsible to:

- Exercise of a high degree of professional care, skill, prudence and diligence in the management of assets under their direction;
- Perform thorough professional analysis and judgment with respect to all investments held in the account;
- Select and dispose of individual securities and related matters;
- Diversify securities by issuer, industry, geography, type, and maturity of investments, etc.;
- Fully comply with all provisions of all governmental regulations and decisions thereunder dealing with the management and investment of foundations; and
- Cooperate with the Foundation on shareholder activities.

Asset Allocation

Assets will be diversified both by asset class (domestic equities, foreign equities, fixed income, venture capital, private placements and real estate) and within each asset class.

Foreign debt and equity securities may include an allocation to emerging market countries. Emerging market securities are defined as those issued by companies based in any except the following countries: Australia, Austria, Belgium, Canada, Denmark, Finland, France, Germany, Hong Kong, Ireland, Italy, Japan, the Netherlands, New Zealand, Norway, Portugal, Singapore, Spain, Sweden, Switzerland, the United Kingdom, and the United States.

The emerging market allocation may be accomplished via the hiring of managers specializing in emerging markets investing or through an allocation within broad foreign portfolios.

Emerging market debt securities should not exceed 20% of the market value of total foreign debt securities. Emerging market equity securities should not exceed 20% of the market value of total emerging market equity securities.

The Foundation does not currently invest in foreign debt securities.

Asset allocation will fall within the following ranges:

Equities   50% to 70%
Fixed Income   20% to 30%
Alternative Investments   5% to 20%

On a quarterly basis, the Foundation's President and Treasurer shall review the over- and under-weighting of the asset allocation and rebalance the assets to bring them in line with policy ranges.

Screening

The Jessie Smith Noyes Foundation views its investments as an integrated component of its overall mission. Investments are based on sound, professional financial analysis and filtered through screens consistent with and in support of the Foundation's values and mission. Exclusionary screens guide managers on companies to avoid and inclusionary screens guide managers on companies in which to invest.

The Foundation's domestic and international equity and fixed income asset classes, held in separate accounts, are managed by investment managers, who use financial analysis and social and environmental screens that match or are greater than those described in this policy.

The Foundation also utilizes socially screened mutual funds. Investments in mutual funds are made even if all of the Foundation's screens are not addressed, provided that the overall orientation of such funds is consistent with the Foundation's mission and values.

Managers are free to choose the sources of data needed to apply the screens. Among the firms doing social investment research are: KLD Research and Analytics, Inc., Institutional Shareholders Services, Investor Responsibility Research Center and Innovest Strategic Value Advisors. Additional sources include reports and information provided by government agencies and advocacy groups and stories found in general, business and trade media. Managers are encouraged to consult with the Foundation if there are questions regarding the screens.

In certain cases, shares may be owned in a company that is incompatible with the Foundation's mission. This provides the Foundation with the option of engaging as an active shareholder with that company.

In order to avail itself of a full spectrum of investment diversification, the Foundation may invest in asset classes where screening is limited or unavailable, including hedge/absolute return funds, venture capital and real estate. To the extent possible, the Foundation will seek to identify and consider managers in these asset classes who include screening in their investment processes and/or ensure that such investments are benign in relation to the Foundation's mission.

The Foundation will review the relationship between financial returns and the impact of screening at least once every three years.

The Foundation has developed specific exclusionary and inclusionary screens for each of its program areas.

Proxy Voting Guidelines

We believe that passive holding of corporate stocks without assessment of the social and environmental, as well as the financial performance of a corporation does not fulfill our obligation as a shareholder. The Foundation asks each of our managers, the Interfaith Center on Corporate Responsibility (ICCR) and the Council of Institutional Investors (CII) to inform us of shareholder resolutions being considered with corporations in which we hold stock. The Foundation votes its proxies as follows:

• When program interests are directly involved, proxies are voted in a manner consistent with them; and

• When a shareholder resolution deals with a social or environmental issue that is not directly related to the Foundation's program interests, the Foundation will review each individual case and consult with our grantees, managers and others, as appropriate.

On issues of corporate governance the Foundation will consult with ICCR, CII, and others, and will vote our proxies according to the following general guidelines:

- Ratify Auditors;
- Ratify Directors unless governance or a program interest issue has been raised or there is a lack of diversity on the board;
- Vote against golden parachutes for executives;
- Vote for proposals requiring a majority of independent directors;
- Vote for proposals requiring nominating and/or compensation committees to be composed exclusively of independent directors;
- Vote against incentive payments not related to financial performance;
- Vote for incentive payments that are tied to social and environmental performance; and
- Vote for proposals recognizing the standing of stakeholders other than shareholders in governance and control.

Monitoring

The Finance Committee will monitor the performance of the Foundation's managers on a quarterly basis, with a face-to-face meeting scheduled at regular intervals.

Performance Standards

Following are the benchmarks against which the Foundation's long-term investment performance is measured. For total Foundation assets and for each asset class a peer group universe benchmark and market index benchmark has been established. It is expected that the aggregate fund and the individual managers will meet or exceed these performance standards on the following bases:

- Absolute returns should exceed both benchmarks on a three- and five-year rolling basis; and
- Risk, as measured by the annualized standard deviation of quarterly returns, should be less than that of the market index over the same three- and five-year rolling periods. Higher volatility is acceptable if the risk-adjusted return, as measured by the Sharpe ratio, is greater than that of the market index.

The peer group manager universe benchmarks are to be composed of professionally managed institutional managers for the Foundation's separate and collective account managers and mutual funds for the Foundation's mutual fund managers. Peer group universes are currently provided by William M. Mercer Investment Consulting, Inc. for separate accounts and Morningstar, Inc. for mutual funds. The market index benchmarks were established in light of the Foundation's financial objectives and long-term expectations for the capital markets and inflation.

Benchmarks

Asset	Peer Group Universe	Market Index
Total Foundation	Endowment/Foundation Universe	N/A
	Blended Target Universe:	**Blended Target Index:**
	48% Equity — 10% International	10% MSCI EAFE (Net) Index
	28% US Large Cap	28% S&P 500 Index
	10% US Small Cap	10% Russell 2000 Index
	25% Fixed Income — Core	24% Lehman Bros. Aggregate Bond Index
	12% Venture Capital — US Equity Combined	1% US 91-Day T-Bills Index
	15% Hedge Funds — US Equity Combined	27% Wilshire 5000 Index
Fixed Income	Core Fixed Income Universe	95% Lehman Bros. Aggregate Bond Index
		5% US 91-Day T-Bills Index
Domestic Equity:		
Large Cap Growth	Large Cap Growth Equity Universe	Domini 400 Social Index, S&P 500 Index
Small Cap	Small Cap Equity Universe	Russell 2000 Growth Index. Russell 2000 Value Index
International Equity	International Equity Universe	MSCI EAFE (Net) Dividend Index
Alternative Investments	N/A	HFRI Fund of Funds Index
		CSFB/Tremont Hedge Fund Index

Manager Review and Termination

Investment funds may be placed on "watch" status, replaced or terminated whenever the Finance Committee loses confidence in the management of the fund, when the characteristics of the fund are no longer consistent with the fund's intended role, or the current style is no longer deemed appropriate.

Conclusion

The Noyes Foundation set out to reduce the dissonance between its grantmaking values and asset management beginning in 1993. Since then we have learned much. We are pleased to share our experience with other foundations that share our concerns for dissonance reduction, and to learn what they are doing, as well. Each year we will report our progress in the Annual Report.

Approved – January 1997.

Revised – March 2001, July 2003, November 2004, November 2005 & November 2006

Note: This is an edited version of the Jessie Smith Noyes Foundation Investment Policy Statement. The complete statement is available at http://www.noyes.org/investpol.html.

Appendix 2:

Mission-Related Investing Financial Consultant Request for Proposal

[Candidate Firm Address]

Dear _____:

The ABC Foundation seeks to hire a financial consultant to manage its financial assets according to mission-related investing ("MRI") principles. [Insert Organization Description with charitable mission, governance structure, etc.]

Financial Resources and Assets to Be Managed
[Insert]

Financial Advisor Scope of Work
The Financial Consultant is requested to provide the following professional investment services and guidance:

1. Develop Investment Policy Statement:
• Work with the ABC board of directors to establish an Investment Policy Statement reflecting its risk tolerance, time horizon, financial return objectives as well as the goal of applying MRI principles to the portfolio.

2. *Initial Asset Allocation and Advisory:*

- Develop initial asset allocations across an appropriate range of domestic and international asset classes, including but not limited to equity, fixed income, cash, and alternative assets.
- Present appropriate, cost-effective account management options (e.g. separately managed accounts, no-load funds, exchange-traded funds, active and passive management.)
- Identify, screen, and recommend appropriate investment managers/vehicles for each asset class and account management option.
- Identify, report, and apply positive and negative MRI screens to investments in appropriate asset classes according to our investment policies.
- Advise us on community investing opportunities such as certificates of deposit with community development financial institutions, community development venture capital funds, microfinance funds, etc.
- Advise and assist us in participating in shareholder advocacy and engagement through stockholder resolutions and other vehicles and organizations.
- Develop appropriate risk management strategies.

3. *Ongoing Monitoring and Reporting:*

- Recommend strategic and tactical changes in asset allocation as appropriate, with face-to-face reviews no less than annually.
- Assess investment performance and submit monthly/quarterly/ annual reports to ABC in agreed-upon, easily accessible formats; be available to consult with staff.
- Recommend, evaluate, and, if necessary, replace third party investment managers.
- Review and recommend changes to the Investment Policy Statement as appropriate in light of external changes in the

overall market or changes in the investment and mission goals of ABC.

The Financial Consultant Selection Process

The selection process will be conducted in three further stages. The ABC Foundation has circulated this Request for Proposal ("RFP") to Y candidate firms. The purpose of this RFP is to help ABC to gain an understanding of the potential financial consultant's capabilities in investment strategy and client service, as well as basic information on the firm's size and structure. Initial RFP responses will be used to compare firms and as resource material for detailed discussions with at least two candidates. Finalists will meet with the ABC Investment Advisory Committee.

If your firm wishes to be considered as a candidate to undertake the Scope of Work outlined in the previous section, please respond to the attached questionnaire. We request that you please answer the questions with detailed information and descriptions rather than "boilerplate" responses. Descriptions of your firm's background, staff, assets under management, and products should include only those capabilities and resources which are relevant to our portfolio and would be readily available to us. This consideration is particularly applicable to candidates from smaller investment units working within large institutions.

We ask you to send either one electronic copy of your proposal or eight hard copies to ABC at the address below for receipt no later than Month/Day/Year.

We greatly appreciate your interest in working with us and look forward to reviewing your proposal. Should you have specific questions about the RFP, please contact [XXX.]

Sincerely yours,

XXXX

Financial Consultant Request for Proposal Questionnaire

Organizational Information
1. Firm Name, Main Address, Other Office Locations;
2. Direct Contact Name of Engagement Leader with Title, Address, Phone and Email; and
3. Direct Contact Name for this RFP with Title, Address, Phone and Email.

Organizational Background
1. When was your firm established? Describe the ownership structure of your firm. Identify affiliated or subsidiary organizations.
2. Clearly identify which office, branch, or subsidiary group within your parent organization would be the primary and lead interface with ABC.
3. How long has your firm provided services such as those described in the Scope of Work?
4. Please attach your firm's financial statement and describe its financial strength.
5. Within the past three years, have there been significant developments in your organization such as a change in ownership, personnel reorganization, or new business ventures? If so, please describe. Do you expect any changes over the next five years?
6. Over the past three years, has your organization or any officer or principal been involved in any litigation or other legal proceedings relating to your investment activities? If so, provide a brief explanation and indicate the current status.
7. Where are regulatory reports, e.g. SEC, about your organization available for our review?

Professional Staff

1. Provide an organizational chart identifying the key professionals in your organization and identify those who would be working on this engagement. How are client relationships managed and how are specific professionals matched with particular clients?
2. Describe the experience and backgrounds of the key investment professionals who would be working on this engagement. Please provide the individual's or individuals' professional biography, including the length of each individual's tenure in the investment industry and with your firm. If applicable, describe the division of the firm for which these engagement leader(s) work.
3. What is the number and size of other clients that the above-listed personnel serve and in what capacity do they serve them? What is the largest number of clients that any of these individuals or teams serve?
4. Indicate any turnover of professional staff over the past three years. What kind of personnel continuity can we expect? If turnover occurs, what processes are in place to maintain relationship and service continuity?

Assets and Accounts Under Management

1. Provide your firm's total assets under management and number of accounts by asset class for the last three years.
2. Provide your firm's total assets under account and number of accounts for the last three years in the following categories: MRI, Community Investing, and Shareholder Advocacy. Please describe how your firm determines and validates its execution of each of the above three categories.
3. What is the size of your largest account in each of these categories?

Investment Strategy and Services

1. What is your experience and approach in developing Investment Policy Statements for nonprofits with an organizational structure such as ours and consisting of community-based board members? What is your experience monitoring such policies?

2. Describe your firm's overall investment philosophy as well as your specific approach to MRI, Community Investing, and Shareholder Advocacy.

3. Does your firm use positive and negative screens or other approaches to MRI? With which asset classes have you used MRI? What are the appropriate benchmarks for these strategies?

4. Describe your firm's investment decision-making process including sell decisions.

5. Describe the structure and organization of your firm's research capability and how it is incorporated into the process. Also describe the integration of any third party research services. How many buy-side research analysts are devoted exclusively to investment management research at your firm?

Investment Performance

1. Please provide your firm's five-year performance data versus the appropriate benchmarks for the asset classes which you expect to use in this portfolio.

2. Please provide three client references. Include client name, address, and name and telephone number of contact person, portfolio size, and length of time managing the account. Pleased be advised that ABC plans to interview these references.

Trading Capabilities

1. Describe your securities trading capabilities and how they would relate to this portfolio.
2. Describe the systems and procedures used to settle, monitor trades, and reconcile accounts with custodians.
3. Describe how your firm minimizes trading costs.
4. Describe your capabilities to structure and execute hedging strategies for concentrated stock positions.

Reporting

1. Please provide sample reports which your firm proposes to use concerning:
   — Investment Policy Statements;
   — Asset Allocation;
   — Performance and Evaluation of investment managers;
   — Investment Returns reporting formats, e.g. net of fees, etc; and
   — Quantitative assessments of portfolio specific investment risks.
2. Describe the asset allocation and performance measurement software your firm utilizes, and specify if it is proprietary or obtained from an outside vendor.
3. Describe the quantitative and qualitative methods your firm employs to evaluate third-party investment managers.
4. Describe any proprietary or third party databases which your firm uses for screening.
5. Describe the format and means through which reports are provided, e.g. on-line, customized letters, statements, printed bulletins, meetings.
6. Describe your client servicing standards and turn-around times.

Standards of Conduct and Fees

ABC wants to provide the only compensation that the firm and any third-party investment managers receive related to the Scope of Work.

1. What are your firm's conflicts of interest, or apparent conflicts of interest, with respect to providing the above-described services to us? How are each of these conflicts disclosed to us and then mitigated?
2. Will the firm accept compensation from any source other than us as a result of providing services to us? If so, describe.
3. Will third-party money managers accept compensation from any other source other than us as a result of providing services to us? If so, describe. If not, how will the firm ensure that they do not?
4. Provide the names and asset values of clients whose relationship with your firm has ended within the past three . years. Why did these relationships end?

Fee Structure

ABC is seeking a transparent fee structure that identifies material cost and expense items rather than an "all-in" fee structure.

1. Describe all proposed fees and costs entailed in your firm's provision of the services outlined in the Scope of Work.
2. Attach a detailed Fee Schedule which clearly identifies all transaction fees and differentiates core fees from optional fees for additional services. Indicate which fees are negotiable or otherwise variable. Fees should be presented as a percentage of assets under management.
3. Describe your billing practices. Does your firm offer discounts for non-profit organizations?
4. Attach a copy of your firm's standard consulting contract and

please indicate if the firm is willing to customize the consulting contract to reflect the needs of ABC. Please be advised that a refusal to negotiate revisions to the standard contract is likely to result in disqualification of the firm.

Sample Portfolio for Fee Calculation

In order to clarify your fee proposal and to compare fees among the candidate financial consultants, we have created the following sample portfolio which represents an estimate of our financial assets. Please provide your **all-in fees** for this portfolio. All fees should be presented as an annual percentage based on assets under management. These fees should also include any expenses for the integration of MRI, community investment, or shareholder engagement strategies.

Source: Godeke Consulting

	Assets Under Management	Advisory Fee	Investment Management Fee	Commissions	Custodial Fees	Other Fees or Charges	Total Fees (BPs)
$X Public Equities:							
Active Equity Manager (U.S.)	$X MM						
Passive Index Manager (U.S.)	$X MM						
Active Equity Manager (International)	$X MM						
Passive Index Manager (International)	$X MM						
Alternatives Asset Classes:	$X MM						
Fixed Income:	$X MM						
Other Assets:	$X MM						
Total	$XXX MM						

Appendix 3:

Due Diligence and Documentation Toolkits for MRI and PRI

The **MRI Evaluator** is designed to work in conjunction with a formal investment due diligence process. It allows a foundation to assess, document and define roles for evaluating any given investment opportunity in the areas of:

• Investment structure, portfolio implications and financial performance reporting;
• Alignment with Mission or Purpose; and
• Establishing Mission "Impact" criteria

Users may be as detailed as they like in documenting the responses to the various questions. Additional comments are included with each set of questions to provide guidance in capturing the most relevant observations.

A scoring system is included for each question, allowing the user to establish a more objective framework for evaluating MRI investments. It is important to document a pass or fail scale for scoring results.

For effective use of the tools, it is important to have a defined mission, documented investment policy and portfolio objectives, established investment due diligence process and a commitment to mission-related investments.

Mission-Related Investment (MRI) Evaluator

Investment Name: _____

Investment Amount Considered: $ _____

Investment Due Diligence by: _____

Signature: _____

Date: _____

Mission Due Diligence by: _____

Signature: _____

Date: _____

Summary Description of Investment:

_____

_____

_____

_____

Main Contacts:

_____

_____

Supporting Documents:

_____

_____

_____

continued

Mission-Related Investment (MRI) Evaluator

Focus Area & Questions	Other Considerations	Score -1/0/+1
Investment Due Diligence (Investment Advisor)		

Investment Structure & Portfolio Implications

Question 1: What investment due diligence process will be required to assess the financial viability of this opportunity?	Foundation's Investment Advisor responsible for performing financial due diligence process.	
Response 1:		
Question 2: What is the structure of the investment under consideration? a. Is the investment structure ideally suited to achieve both the appropriate risk adjusted rate of return and Mission Impact?	Direct public or private, Fund or Fund of Funds. Consider structure's ability to offer sufficient or appropriate diversification to mitigate risk. Consider investment cost structure's implication on Mission Impact.	
Response 2:		
Question 3: What is the asset class? a. Does the investment fall outside the currently established asset allocation targets of the Foundation? b. If so, has the appropriate analysis been completed to evaluate a change in targets? c. Has this change been accepted and adopted under the investment policy guidelines of the Foundation?	While it is the intent of the Foundation to pursue MRIs, there is also a firm commitment to remain within the established investment policy guidelines and risk budget.	
Response 3:		
Question 4: Will members of the Foundation play an active role in the investment? a. If so, will questions of self-dealing arise? b. Should the investment be considered in conjunction with a Foundation grant? c. Outside the Foundation?	Consider additional Mission Impact, regulatory concerns or sizing constraints.	
Response 4:		

Mission-Related Investment (MRI) Evaluator

Focus Area & Questions	Other Considerations	Score -1/0/+1

Investment Due Diligence (Investment Advisor) *continued*

Investment Monitoring & Reporting

Question 5:
What is the financial benchmark that will be used to evaluate this investment?
a. Over what period(s) of time will we measure the investment performance?

Other Considerations: Investment benchmarks are established by the investment due diligence process. Similar to investments made without regard to Mission Impact, investment performance is reported when available and as appropriate for the investment structures and/or asset class.

Response 5:

Mission Due Diligence (Foundation Directors & Philanthropic Advisors)

Mission Alignment

Question 6:
How does this investment align with the Mission of the Foundation?
a. In what area(s) does the Foundation believe this investment will contribute the greatest degree of Mission impact?

Other Considerations: Identify specifically how this investment will impact the Foundation's Mission.

Response 6:

Question 7:
Are there any elements of this investment which are contrary to any value(s) of the Foundation?
a. If so, how is this being addressed?

Other Considerations: Evaluate potential tradeoffs.

Response 7:

Relationship & Reputation

Question 8:
How well does the Foundation know the investment and/or strategy?
a. What is the nature and duration of this relationship?
b. Have members of the Foundation made site visit(s)?

Other Considerations: Document personal and direct understanding of the investment strategy by the Foundation.

Response 8:

© Raúl Pomares 2008; additional contributors Doug Bauer of Rockefeller Philanthropy Advisors and Charly and Lisa Kleissner of the KL Felicitas Foundation.

Mission-Related Investment (MRI) Evaluator

Focus Area & Questions	Other Considerations	Score -1/0/+1

Mission Due Diligence (Foundation Directors & Philanthropic Advisors) *cont.*

Relationship & Reputation *continued*

Question 9: Have other foundations or investors recognized this as an MRI or social investment? a. Do other respected partners of the Foundation have a relationship with or experience with this investment?	Capture any peer or trusted partner knowledge on the investment.	
Response 9:		
Question 10: How integral to the success of the investment is the Mission Impact? a. How much personal financial capital have the investment principals and/or founders committed to the investment?	Identify alignment of interest by investment principals and/or founders.	
Response 10:		

Mission Impact Monitoring & Reporting

Question 11: What approach will be used to evaluate the Mission Impact of the investment? a. What is the proposed nature and scale of the Mission Impact, e.g. in 1 year, 3 years, long term?	Pre-established metrics and evaluation intervals for Social or Mission Impact should be requested or developed.	
Response 11:		
Question 12: Will the Investment Manager provide Mission related reporting?	Once Mission criteria are established it is important to communicate with the Investment Manager and determine if the criteria can be met.	
Response 12:		
Question 13: Does the investment scale, accelerate, support or re-enforce other SMSIs in the investment or grant portfolios?	Identify those that will be impacted and evaluate excess or leveraged Mission Impact.	
Response 13:		

Mission-Related Investment (MRI) Evaluator
Additional Comments or Observations

The **PRI Evaluator** is designed to work in conjunction with a formal investment due diligence process. It allows a foundation to assess, document and define roles for evaluating any given investment opportunity in the areas of:

- Documentation of PRI status for IRS compliance;
- Alignment with Program and/or Mission;
- Investment structure, portfolio implications and financial performance reporting; and
- Establishing Program "Impact" criteria

Users may be as detailed as they like in documenting the responses to the various questions. Additional comments are included with each set of questions to provide guidance in capturing the most relevant observations.

A scoring system is included for each question, allowing the user to establish a more objective framework for evaluating PRI investments. It is important to document a pass or fail scale for scoring results.

For effective use of the tools, it is important to have a defined Program/Mission, documented investment policy and portfolio objectives, established investment due diligence process and a commitment to Program-Related Investments.

Program-Related Investment (PRI) Evaluator

Investment Name: _____

Investment Amount Considered: $ _____

Investment Due Diligence by: _____

Signature: _____

Date: _____

Program Due Diligence by: _____

Signature: _____

Date: _____

Summary Description of Investment:

_____

_____

_____

_____

Main Contacts:

_____

_____

Supporting Documents:

_____

_____

_____

_____

Program-Related Investment (PRI) Evaluator

Focus Area & Questions	Other Considerations	Score -1/0/+1

Program Due Diligence (Foundation Directors & Philanthropic Advisors)

IRS Compliance

Question 1: Is this investment compliant with the definition of PRI in the Tax Reform Act of 1969 section 4944? a. Is its primary purpose to advance the Foundation's charitable objectives? b. Is the primary purpose income production or property appreciation? c. Will funds be used either directly or indirectly to lobby or for political purposes?	If not compliant, then not eligible to be a PRI. Foundation can consider a grant, MRI or other investment as appropriate.	

Response 1:

Program Alignment

Question 2: How does this investment align with Programs of the Foundation? a. In what area(s) does the Foundation believe this investment will contribute the greatest degree of Program Impact?	Identify specifically how this investment will impact the Foundation's Programs.	

Response 2:

Question 3: Are there any elements of this investment which are contrary to any value(s) of the Foundation? a. If so, how is this addressed?	Evaluate potential tradeoffs.	

Response 3:

Question 4: What conditions exist that suggest this PRI is a more effective or appropriate vehicle for achieving the Foundation's programmatic objectives versus a grant?	Evaluate the capital market environment or lack thereof for such an investment.	

Response 4:

© Raúl Pomares 2008; additional contributors Doug Bauer of Rockefeller Philanthropy Advisors and Charly and Lisa Kleissner of the KL Felicitas Foundation.

Program-Related Investment (PRI) Evaluator

Focus Area & Questions	Other Considerations	Score -1/0/+1

Program Due Diligence (Foundation Directors & Philanthropic Advisors) *cont.*

Relationship and Reputation

Question 5: How well does the Foundation know the investment and/or strategy? a. What is the nature and duration of this relationship? b. Have members of the Foundation made site visit(s)?	Document personal and direct understanding of the investment strategy by the Foundation.	
Response 5:		
Question 6: Have other Foundations recognized this as a PRI or social investment? a. Do other respected partners of the foundation have a relationship with or experience with this investment?	Capture any peer or trusted partner knowledge on the investment.	
Response 6:		
Question 7: What is the form and level of personal commitment by the investment principals and/or founders to the Programmatic Impact of the investment?	Identify alignment of interest by investment principals and/or founders.	
Response 7:		

Program Impact Monitoring & Reporting

Question 8: What approach will be used to evaluate the Program Impact of the investment? a. What is the proposed nature and scale of the Program Impact, e.g. in 1 year, 3 years, long term?	Pre-established metrics and evaluation intervals for Program Impact should be requested or developed.	
Response 8:		
Question 9: Will the Investment Manager provide Program related reporting?	Once Program criteria are established it is important to communicate with the Investment Manager and determine if criteria can be met.	
Response 9:		

Appendix 3: Toolkits for MRI and PRI

Program-Related Investment (PRI) Evaluator

Focus Area & Questions	Other Considerations	Score -1/0/+1

Program Due Diligence (Foundation Directors & Philanthropic Advisors) *cont.*

Program Impact Monitoring & Reporting *continued*

Question 10:
Does the investment scale, accelerate, support or re-enforce other SMSIs in the investment or grant portfolios?

Identify those that will be impacted and evaluate excess or leveraged Program Impact.

Response 10:

Investment Due Diligence (Investment Advisor)

Investment Structure & Portfolio Implications

Question 11:
What investment due diligence process will be required to assess the financial viability of this opportunity?

Foundation Investment Advisor responsible for performing financial due diligence process upon completion of PRI evaluator.

Response 11:

Question 12:
What is the structure of the investment under consideration?
a. Is the investment structure ideally suited to achieve both the appropriate risk adjusted rate of return (within 500 basis points of similar investments made without regard to program considerations) and Program Impact?

Direct public or private, Fund or Fund of Funds. Consider structure's ability to offer sufficient or appropriate diversification to mitigate risk. Consider investment cost structure's implication on Program Impact.

Response 12:

Question 13:
What is the asset class?
a. Does the investment fall outside of the currently established asset allocation targets of the Foundation?
b. If so, has the appropriate analysis been completed to evaluate a change in targets?
c. Has this change been accepted and adopted under the investment policy guidelines of the Foundation?

While it is the intent of the Foundation to pursue PRIs, there is also a firm commitment to remain within the established investment policy guidelines and risk budget.

Response 13:

Program-Related Investment (PRI) Evaluator

Focus Area & Questions	Other Considerations	Score -1/0/+1

Investment Due Diligence (Investment Advisor) *cont.*

Investment Structure & Portfolio Implications *continued*

Question 14: Will members of the Foundation play an active role in the investment? a. If so, will questions of self-dealing arise? b. Should the investment be considered in conjunction with a Foundation grant? c. Outside the Foundation?	Consider additional Program Impact, regulatory concerns or sizing constraints.	

Response 14:

Investment Monitoring & Reporting

Question 15: What is the investment benchmark that will be used to evaluate this investment? Over what period(s) of time will we measure the investment performance?	Investment benchmarks are established by the investment due diligence process based on similar investments made without regard to Program Impact. Investment performance is reported when available and as appropriate for the investment structures and/or asset class.	

Response 15:

Additional Comments or Observations

© Raúl Pomares 2008; additional contributors Doug Bauer of Rockefeller Philanthropy Advisors and Charly and Lisa Kleissner of the KL Felicitas Foundation.

Appendix 4:
Mission-Related Investment Scoring Questionnaire

Program Impact	Financial Risk/Return
How relevant is this investment to current program priorities?	*How will the project benefit specifically from an investment rather than another type of financial support?*
To what extent does this investment further and help inform existing program work?	
	Is the project financially sustainable?
To what degree does this investment leverage existing relationships and knowledge within the sponsoring program area?	*What is the likelihood of getting capital back?*
To what degree can this investment help connect the program area to value-added relationships?	*What level of financial return can we realistically expect?*
	Is the expected level of financial return adequate given the degree of risk involved?
Does this investment have the potential to create a model that would contribute toward program goals?	
	Will the field benefit from application of this financial structure?
To what extent will this investment generate learning that will be useful for other program areas?	

Appendix 5:
Impact Value Chain

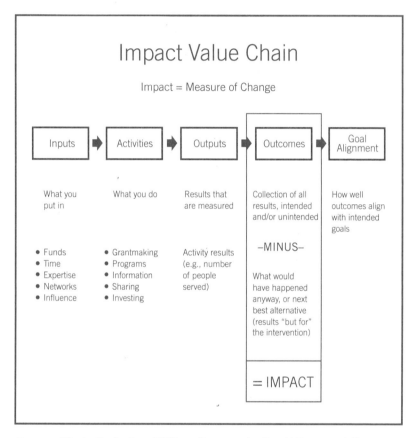

Source: *Clark, Catherine, William Rosenzweig, David Long, and Sara Olsen,* Double Bottom Line Project Report: Assessing Social Impact in Double Bottom Line Ventures, *The Rockefeller Foundation, 2004.*

Resources/ Bibliography

Ambachtsheer, Jane, Global Head of SRI Mercer Investment Consulting Toronto, "Socially Responsible Investing," Benefits & Compensation International, Volume 35, Number 1 July/August 2005.

Anderson, Miranda, and David Gardiner, "Managing the Risks and Opportunities of Climate Change: a Practical Toolkit for Corporate Leaders," Boston, MA: CERES, 2006.

Bishop, Matthew, "The Business of Giving," The Economist, 25 February 2006.

"Blended Value Investing: Capital Opportunities for Social and Environmental Impact," World Economic Forum, Geneva, Switzerland, 2006.

Bolton, Margaret, "Foundations and Social Investment: Making Money Work Harder," Esmée Fairbairn Foundation, October 2005.

Brody Weiser Burns, "Program-Related Investments for Small Foundations," Association of Small Foundations 2004 National Conference, 16 October 2004.

Bruck, Connie, "Millions for Millions," The New Yorker, 30 October 2006, pp. 62-73.

Building Tools for Effective Philanthropy, Washington, DC, PRI Makers Network.

Carlson, Neil, "Assessing and Managing PRI Risk: Nothing Ventured, Nothing Gained," Grantcraft, 2006.

Chan, Margaret, "Address to 60th World Health Assembly," World Health Organization, Geneva, Switzerland, 15 May 2007.

Clark, Catherine, William Rosenzweig, David Long, and Sara Olsen, Double Bottom Line Project Report: Assessing Social Impact in Double Bottom Line Ventures, The Rockefeller Foundation, 2004.

Cogan, Douglas G., Corporate Governance and Climate Change: Making the Connection, Investor Responsibility Research Center, Boston, MA: CERES, 2006.

Cooch, Sarah, Mark Kramer, Fi Cheng, Adeeb Mahmud, Ben Marx, and Matthew Rehrig, Compounding Impact: Mission Investing by U.S. Foundations, FSG Social Impact Advisors, Boston, MA, 2007.

Cooch, Sarah and Mark Kramer, Aggregating Impact: A Foundation's Guide to U.S. Mission Investment Intermediaries, FSG Social Impact Advisors, Boston, MA, 2007.

"Creating Social Capital Markets for Fourth Sector Organizations: Opportunities and Challenges," 14 June 2007, Google, New York, 2007.

Davis, Lee, Nicole Etchart, and Claire Costello, "All in the Same Boat: an Introduction to Engaged Philanthropy," ed. Edith Goldenhar, Nonprofit Enterprise and Self-Sustainability Team. NESsT, 2005.

Deutsch, Claudia H., "Study Says U.S. Companies Lag on Global Warming," The New York Times, 22 March 2006.

Dietel, William M., "Mission Stewardship: Aligning Programs, Investments, and Administration to Achieve Impact," The F.B. Heron Foundation, 2007.

Dunn, Brian, "Alternative Investment Opportunities Offering Financial Return and Social Impact," August 2006, Aquillian Investments, San Francisco, CA, 2006.

Easton, Tom, "The Hidden Wealth of the Poor," The Economist, 5 November 2005.

Emerson, Jed and Tim Little, with Jonas Kron, "The Prudent Trustee: The Evolution of the Long-Term Investor," Generation Foundation and the Rose Foundation for Communities and the Environment, 2005.

Emerson, Jed and Joshua Spitzer, "From Fragmentation to Function: Critical Concepts and Writings on Social Capital Markets' Structure, Operation and Innovation," Skoll Centre for Social Entrepreneurship, 2007.

Emerson, Jed, Joshua Spitzer and Jacob Harold, "Blended Value Investing: Innovations in Real Estate," Skoll Centre for Social Entrepreneurship, 2007.

Emerson, Jed, Shari Berenbach and Timothy Freundlich, "Where Money Meets Mission: Creating a Unified Investment Strategy," 2007.

Environmental Impact, CERES, 2004.

Esposito, Virginia M., ed. et al, Splendid Legacy: The Guide to Creating Your Family Foundation, National Center for Family Philanthropy, 2002.

EuroSIF, Pension Programme SRI Toolkit, 2004.

Fitzgerald, Niall, and Mandy Cormack, The Role of Business in Society: an Agenda for Action, The Conference Board, Harvard University Kennedy School of Government, and the International Business Leaders Forum, 2007, pp. 4-36.

Fleishman, Joel L., The Foundation: A Great American Secret: How Private Wealth is Changing the World, PublicAffairs, 2007.

Freshfields Bruckhaus Deringer, Legal Framework for the Integration of Environmental, Social and Governance Issues into Institutional Investment, 2005. (http://www.unepfi.org/fileadmin/documents/freshfields_legal_resp _20051123.pdf.)

Gary, Tracy, "Giving Families, Giving Communities," 10 November 2004.

Giller, Chip, trans., "How Green is Your Cash?" Contribute New York, February-March 2007: pp. 42-45.

Godeke, Steven, "Hybrid Transactions in the US Social Capital Market," Alliance Magazine, September 2006, (www.alliancemagazine.org).

Goldman Sachs Global Strategy Research, "The Growing Interest in Environmental Issues is Important to Both Socially Responsible and Fundamental Investors," August 2005.

Goodman, Sandra, and Michael Walker, Benchmarking Air Emissions of the 100 Largest Electric Power Producers in the United States, CERES, NRDC, PSEG. CERES, NRDC, PSEG, 2006.

Gore, Al, and David Blood, "For People and Planet," The Wall Street Journal, 28 March 2006.

Gunther, Marc, "Global Warming Could Melt Your Portfolio," Fortune, 21 March 2006.

Gunther, Marc, "Warren Buffet and Darfur," Fortune, 20 April 2007.

Haboucha, Farha-Joyce, Focus on Climate Change, Socially Responsive Investing, 15 December 2006, Rockefeller & Co., Inc., 2006.

Hagerman, Lisa A., Gordon L. Clark, and Tessa Hebb, "Massachusetts Pension Reserves Investment Management Board: Urban Investing through a Transparent Selection Process," Labor & Worklife Program, Harvard Law School, August 2007.

Hawken, Paul, "Socially Responsible Investment," The Natural Capital Institute, October 2004.

Heller, Jonathan A.G., "Dissecting the Benefits of Socially Responsible Investing," Family Office Forum, June 2007.

"Hey, Is It Hot in Here?" Pensions & Investments, 1 May 2006.

Humphreys, Josh, comp. The Social Responsiveness of Philanthropic Foundations: Long-Term Perspectives, The Rockefeller University, 2007.

"Introduction to Social Investing," Best Practices for Foundations, 6 June 2006, FPCR, <www.foundationpartnership.org/BestPract.htm>.

"Investing in One World," Microvest, 2005.

Johnson, Kyle, "Social Investing," Cambridge Associates LLC, 2007.

Kinder, Peter, "The Virtue of Consistency: The Gates Foundation & Mission-Related Investing," 2007.

Kramer, Mark, and Sarah Cooch, Investing for Impact, FSG Social Impact Advisors, Boston, MA, 2006.

La Franchi, Debbie, and Belden Daniels, State of the Industry: Double Bottom Line Funds, Economic Innovation International, Inc., Los Angeles, CA, 2006.

Lash, Jonathan, and Fred Wellington, "Competitive Advantage on a Warming Planet," Harvard Business Review, March 2007, pp. 3-13.

Lewis, Jonathan C. and Robert A. Wexler, "Mission Investing in Microfinance: A Program Related Investment (PRI) Primer and Toolkit," Microcredit Enterprises, July 2007.

Lipman, Harvey, "Meshing Proxy with Mission: Few Foundations Do Much to Influence Shareholder Votes," Chronicle of Philanthropy, May 4, 2006.

Lufkin, Elise, Mission-Related Investing for Foundations and Non-Profit Organizations: Practical Tools for Mission/Investment Integration, Trillium Asset Management, Boston, 2007.

Lydenberg, Steven D., "Envisioning Socially Responsible Investing," Domini Social Investments, 2002.

Mackerron, Conrad, ed., Douglas Bauer and Michael Passoff, Unlocking the Power of the Proxy, New York, NY, Rockefeller Philanthropy Advisors and The As You Sow Foundation, 2004.

Mainstreaming Responsible Investment, World Economic Forum, Geneva, 2005.

The Materiality of Social, Environmental and Corporate Governance Issues to Equity Pricing, UNEP Finance Initiative, Asset Management Working Group, June 2004.

McGray, Douglas, "Network Philanthropy," The Los Angeles Times, 21 January 2007.

"Measuring Social Impact: The Foundation of Social Return on Investment," London Business School and the New Economics Foundation, 2006.

Mendonca, Lenny T. and Jeremy Oppenheim, "Investing in Sustainability: An Interview with Al Gore and David Blood," The McKinsey Quarterly, May 2007.

Mercer Investment Consulting, "2006 Fearless Forecast: What Do Investment Managers Think About Responsible Investment?" Mercer Investment Consulting, 2006.

Miller, Clara, "The Looking-Glass World of Nonprofit Money: Managing in For-Profits' Shadow Universe," The Nonprofit Quarterly, Spring 2005.

National Committee for Responsive Philanthropy, "A Call for Mission-Based Investing by America's Private Foundations," September 2005.

"New Journey: Aligning Investment with Mission at the Northwest Area Foundation," Northwest Area Foundation, undated brochure.

Orlitzky, Marc, Frank L. Schmidt, and Sara L. Rynes, Corporate Social and Financial Performance: A Meta Analysis, Social Investment Forum Foundation, Washington, D.C., 2004.

Olsen, Sara and Woody Tasch, "Mission-Related Investing: A Workshop for Foundations," Investors Circle Foundation, 2003.

Penna, Robert M. and William J. Phillips, Outcome Frameworks, An Overview for Practitioners, 2005.

Piller, Charles, "Foundations Align Investments with their Charitable Goals," The Los Angeles Times, 29 December 2007.

Porter, Michael E. and Mark R. Kramer, "Philanthropy's New Agenda: Creating Value," Harvard Business Review, November–December 1999, pp. 121-130.

Price, Tom, Activists in the Boardroom: How Advocacy Groups Seek to Shape Corporate Behavior, Foundation for Public Affairs, Washington, D.C., 2006.

"Private Investment for Social Goals: Building the Blended Value Capital Market," World Economic Forum, Geneva, Switzerland, 2005.

"Program-Related Investing: Skills & Strategies for New PRI Funders," Grantcraft, 2006.

Proxy Season Preview: Helping Foundations Align Mission and Investment, Rockefeller Philanthropy Advisors, New York, 2007.

Questions and Answers for Foundations on Proxy Voting, CERES, 2006.

"Real Estate PRI Case Study: Hollywood Community Housing Corporation," San Francisco, CA: Neighborhood Funders Group, 2007.

The Roberts Enterprise Development Fund, SROI Reports, San Francisco, CA, 2000.

Social Investment Forum, "The Mission in the Marketplace: How Responsible Investing Can Strengthen the Fiduciary Oversight of Foundation Endowments and Enhance Philanthropic Missions," 2007.

"Social Purpose Capital Market: An Opportunity for the Canadian Charitable Sector," Tides Canada Foundation, January 2007.

Southern New Hampshire University, School of Community Economic Development, "Expanding Philanthropy: Mission-Related Investing at the F.B. Heron Foundation," 2007.

Swack, Micheal, Jack Northrup, and Janet Prince, Expanding Philanthropy, School of Community Economic Development, Southern New Hampshire University, Altrushare Securities, 2007.

Vidal, David J., "Reward Trumps Risk: How Business Perspectives on Corporate Citizenship and Sustainability are Changing," The Conference Board Executive Action Series 216th ser. (2006).

Ward, Sally K. Ph.D., Charlie French, Ph.D. and Kelly Giraud, Ph.D., "Building Value and Security for Homeowners in Mobile Home Parks: A Report on Economic Outcomes," The Carsey Institute at the University of New Hampshire, 2006.

Wilhelm, Ian, "Corporate Giving Rebounds," The Chronicle of Philanthropy, August 2005.

Williams, Harold S., Arthur Y. Webb and William J. Phillips, Outcome Funding, A New Approach to Targeted Grantmaking, 1996.

Wood, David and Belinda Hoff, "Handbook on Responsible Investment Across Asset Classes," The Institute of Responsible Investing at the Boston College Center for Corporate Citizenship, 2007.

Zimet, Joseph, "US Philanthropy in the 21st Century: a Driving Force in the Landscape of Aid?" Annual Bank Conference on Development Economics, Tokyo, 29 May 2006.

About the Authors

STEVEN GODEKE
Principal, Godeke Consulting
www.godekeconsulting.com

STEVEN GODEKE is an independent investment advisor who works with foundations, corporations, and non-profit organizations to integrate their financial and philanthropic goals. Based on the desire to link his financial expertise and public policy experience, he founded Godeke Consulting in 2001. Steven advises his clients on the creation and execution of mission-related investment strategies across asset classes and program areas. His clients include The Rockefeller Foundation, The Robin Hood Foundation, The Conference Board, The F.B. Heron Foundation, The Altman Foundation, Common Ground, The World Economic Forum and corporate clients in the financial services and pharmaceutical industries. Steven is an adjunct professor at New York University's Center for Global Affairs where he teaches a course in Microfinance and Social Entrepreneurship.

Prior to establishing his own firm, Steven worked for twelve years in corporate and project finance with Deutsche Bank where he structured debt and equity products and advised corporate clients in the telecommunications, media, real estate and natural resources industries. In addition to his business line and client management responsibilities, he was also a member of the bank's strategic planning team. Steven grew up on a family farm in Southern Indiana, and attended Purdue University where he received a B.S. in Management and a B.A. in German.

He studied as a Fulbright Scholar at the University of Cologne and earned an M.P.A. from Harvard University. He currently lives in New York City.

DOUG BAUER
Senior Vice President, Rockefeller Philanthropy Advisors

DOUG BAUER leads the Rockefeller Philanthropy Advisors' Strategic Initiatives Team. Prior to joining RPA in March 2002, he was a Vice President at Goldman Sachs and President of the Goldman Sachs Philanthropy Fund, the firm's charitable giving vehicle. From 1997 to 2000, Doug was Director of Community Partnership at SmithKline Beecham (now GlaxoSmithKline) and Executive Director of the SmithKline Beecham Foundation, where he focused on community-based health care around the world. From 1992 to 1996, Doug was a Program Officer for Culture at the Pew Charitable Trusts. And from 1988 to 1992, he managed the Scott Paper Company Foundation.

Doug's opinions and ideas on philanthropy have been featured in the Associated Press, *The Christian Science Monitor*, *The Chronicle of Philanthropy*, *Contribute*, the *Financial Times*, the *Los Angeles Times*, *The New York Post* and on CNBC. He chairs The Better Business Bureau's Wise Giving Alliance and the Support Center for Nonprofit Management, and serves on the boards or committees for The Carbon Disclosure Project (UK), Children's Health Fund, and NYRAG. He is also an adjunct faculty member at the University of Pennsylvania where he teaches a course and seminars on philanthropy. Doug is a graduate of Michigan State University. He also holds a M.S. from Penn and a M.J. from Temple University.